READING RUTH IN ASIA

Society of Biblical Literature

International Voices in Biblical Studies

Jione Havea, General Editor
Monica J. Melanchthon, General Editor

Editorial Board:
Eric Anum
Ida Fröhlich
Hisako Kinukawa
Néstor Miguez
Aliou C. Niang
Nasili Vaka'uta

Number 7

READING RUTH IN ASIA

Edited by
Jione Havea and Peter H. W. Lau

SBL Press
Atlanta

Copyright © 2015 by SBL Press

All rights reserved. No part of this work may be reproduced or transmitted in any form or by any means, electronic or mechanical, including photocopying and recording, or by means of any information storage or retrieval system, except as may be expressly permitted by the 1976 Copyright Act or in writing from the publisher. Requests for permission should be addressed in writing to the Rights and Permissions Office, SBL Press, 825 Houston Mill Road, Atlanta, GA 30329 USA.

Library of Congress Control Number: 2015953315

Printed on acid-free paper.

Contents

Abbreviations	vii
Preface	ix
Reading Ruth Again, in Asia *Jione Havea* and *Peter H. W. Lau*	1
Another Postcolonial Reading of the Book of Ruth *Peter H.W. Lau*	15
The Key to Successful Migration? Rereading Ruth's Confession (1:16–17) through the Lens of Bhabha's Mimicry *Sin-lung Tong*	35
"Who Is More to You than Seven Sons": A Cross-Textual Reading between the Book of Ruth and *A Pair of Peacocks to the Southeast Fly* *Yan Lin*	47
A Reinterpretation of Levirate Marriage in Ruth 4:1–12 for Kachin Society *Roi Nu*	57
An Intertextual Reading of Ruth and Proverbs 31:10–31, with a Chinese Woman's Perspective *Elaine W. F. Goh*	73
Patriarchy, a Threat to Human Bonding: Reading the Story of Ruth in the Light of Marriage and Family Structures in India *Surekha Nelavala*	89
The Boaz Solution: Reading Ruth in Light of Australian Asylum Seeker Discourse *Anthony Rees*	99
Stirring Naomi: Another Gleaning at the Edges of Ruth 1 *Jione Havea*	111
Bibliography	125
List of contributors	139

Ancient Sources Index 141
Modern Author Index 145

ABBREVIATIONS

AB	Anchor Bible
ABD	*Anchor Bible Dictionary*
BDB	*The Brown-Driver-Briggs Hebrew and English Lexicon*
Bib	*Biblica*
BibInt	*Biblical Interpretation*
BT	*Bible Translator*
BZAW	*Beihefte zur Zeitschrift für die alttestamentliche Wissenschaft*
CBQ	*Catholic Biblical Quarterly*
EN	Ezra-Nehemiah
EvQ	*The Evangelical Quarterly*
HALOT	*Hebrew and Aramaic Lexicon of the Old Testament*
HB	Hebrew Bible
IFJ	International Federation of Journalists
IVP	InterVarsity Press
JBL	*Journal of Biblical Literature*
JHS	*Journal of Hebrew Scruotures*
JJS	*Journal of Jewish Studies*
JOTT	*Journal for Translation and Textlinguistics*
JSOT	*Journal for the Study of the Old Testament*
JSOTSupp	*Journal for the Study of the Old Testament Supplement*
NAC	New American Commentary
NCBC	New Cambridge Bible Commentary
NICOT	New International Commentary on the Old Testament
NSBT	New Studies in Biblical Theology
RN	Ruth narrative
SABS	Society of Asian Biblical Studies
SBL	Society of Biblical Literature
SJOT	*Scandinavian Journal of the Old Testament*
TDOT	Theological Dictionary of the Old Testament
TJ	*Trinity Journal*
TWOT	*Theological Wordbook of the Old Testament*
VT	*Vetus Testamentum*
WBC	Word Bible Commentary
ZAW	*Zeitschrift für die alttestamentliche Wissenschaft*

Preface

The seeds for this collection of essays were sown during the 2012 meeting of the Society of Asian Biblical Studies (SABS) at Sabah Theological Seminary, Kotakinabalu, Malaysia (13–15 June). A lot of the conversations around mealtimes and the breaks circled around the story and the book of Ruth, and so we asked several participants for contributions. As with most book projects, many people were interested but over time the enthusiasm of some died down. Put another way, not all who wanted to glean for this book project came to the field. Nonetheless, other contributors (who did not attend the Malaysia meeting) came to the threshing floor.

Except for the essay by Sin-lung Tong (chapter 3), which is a revision of his article published in *CMS Journal* [Chinese Mission Seminary] 13 (2013): 57–73 and published here with the permission of the journal editor, the other essays have not been published before.

We offer this collection together with an invitation for other collections that engage in regionally based studies, and for seeking to understand what it means, and what is involved, in reading biblical texts in lived contexts, in Asia and yonder.

Jione Havea and Peter H. W. Lau
13 April 2015

READING RUTH AGAIN, IN ASIA

Jione Havea and *Peter H. W. Lau*

Migration exposes the porous nature of borders: borders are holey. As people move with their ways, languages and belongings into the domains of others—like when Elimelech and Naomi moved with their sons in search of refuge in Moab (Ruth 1)—borders are crossed and at once opened. The crossing and the opening of borders coincide: to cross is to open. The borders of Moab and Judah remained open several years later, when Naomi returned with Ruth.

One of the upshots of migration is that, especially when the entry of the newcomers (foreigners) is intrusive and invasive, the drive to secure borders heightens. Something about the presence and appearance of foreigners unnerve locals. Locals do not always know how to deal with people who are foreign and different. We therefore expect anxiety among the local peoples of Moab when Naomi and her family arrived, but the narrator does not bother to explain. When Naomi returned without the men in her family but with a foreign woman on her side, we expect the locals in Judah to find Naomi's arrival as strange and Ruth as foreign.

The holey-ness of borders raises questions about the limits of nations.[1] Since borders are open, where does one nation end and the next begin? This question leads to other questions that echo Gayatri Chakravorty Spivak's affirmation that "there is no nation before nationalism":[2] Is a nation delimited by its land-, ocean-, and air-space or by the ideologies that define it? What about instances when the cultures that arise out of one nation influence the cultures of other, foreign, nations? Is nationalism possible without transnationalism? These

---

[1] The holeyness of borders invites rethinking the connotations of "margin" and "minority" that have been some of the motivations for subaltern and liberation studies. See e.g., essays in R. S. Sugirtharajah, ed., *Still at the Margins: Biblical Scholarship Fifteen Years after Voices from the Margin* (New York: T&T Clark, 2008).

[2] Gayatri Chakravorty Spivak, "Nationalism and the Imagination," *Lectora* 15 (2009): 79 (75–98).

questions apply to the nations of the current times, but we imagine that the same questions apply to nations of generations past.

Where, for instance, are the limits of China? Or more appropriately, can China be closed off by its national borders? These are crucial questions given the presence of China in Hong Kong, Taiwan, and Singapore, as well as in Chinatowns, shops, markets, and households all over the world. Which part of the world does not have evidences of (something) being "made in China"? Where does China end? This cluster of questions may be raised with regard to other nations also, like Egypt and Rome, Bangladesh and Brazil, as well as to regions, like Europe, America, Africa, Oceania, Caribbean, and Asia.

Asia(n)?

Where does Asia begin and end? The origin of the term "Asia" is uncomplimentary. The Italian Jesuit Matteo Ricci coined "Asia" from the Chinese characters *yaxiya*, which means "inferior."[3] With China at the center, *yaxiya*/Asia refers to surrounding inferior peoples who did not belong to China. In the beginning, therefore, China was not part of *yaxiya*/Asia and the neighbors of China did not know the insult of being known as part of "Asia."

In the last four hundred years, "Asia" has lost its insult and instead taken up geographical and cultural designations. In this shift, Asia is known to be so diverse and complex, culturally and religiously,[4] that it cannot be reduced to a simple and unified entity. In terms of geography and cultural diversity, it would be appropriate to speak of four Asias—West Asia, Central Asia, East Asia, and South Asia—but our intention here is not to map or fix the limits of Asia but to call attention to the problems in trying to determine national and regional limits.

Asia cannot be contained, as if it can only refer to the Orient or to the East (as seen from the West). Asia flows into Egypt and Africa,[5] as well as into Oceania, also referred to as the Asia-Pacific region. This raises more questions: If the Pacific, as Spivak observed, is the "absent" part

---

[3] R.S. Sugirtharajah, *The Bible and Asia: From the Pre-Christian Era to the Postcolonial Age* (Cambridge: Harvard University Press, 2013), 2.
[4] See e.g., Philip Chia, "Biblical Studies in a Rising Asia: An Asian Perspective on the Future of the Biblical Past," in *The Future of the Biblical Past: Envisioning Biblical Studies in a Global Key,* ed. Roland Boer and Fernando F. Segovia (Atlanta: Society of Biblical Literature, 2012), 83–90 (81–95).
[5] Sugirtharajah, *Bible and Asia*, 2.

(over which people fly) of the Asia-Pacific,[6] then can the region be whole without the Pacific? Put another way, is Asia complete without the Pacific? Jione Havea's contribution to this collection (chapter 9) presumes that the Pacific makes a difference. Havea brings Naomi into the spotlight in his reading of Ruth 1, drawing on two locations (Moab and Judah) and reading for the people who belong in these places. He also draws on his Tongan heritage to bring insights into biblical text. Some of the experiences and customs he addresses include those related to migration, family relations, and eating.

Another question is this: Does Australia belong in the Asia-Pacific?[7] Anthony Rees's contribution (chapter 8) wrestles with this question. Rees considers the topic of migration by placing Ruth's migration beside the current debate about asylum seekers in Australia. Rees argues that since Asia's geographical and identity boundaries are fluid, this openness invites discussion about Australia's place in Asia. Havea and Rees situate the Pacific and Australia as part of Asia, and their border crossing suggestions reflect the *yaxiya* roots of "Asia" (nations that are outside). In this regard, the Asia supposed in this collection of essays has holey limits.

Contextual and Area studies make attention to Asia (qua region) necessary, but this is easier said than done. Two questions lurk behind the surface: "Which Asia?" and "Whose Asia?" The first question appeals to geographical and ideological opinions, and the second is tied to the matters of identity and location (hence the need to find home[8]). One expects people *in* Asian homelands to define Asia differently as compared to Asians living *outside* from Asia. Migration complexifies this expectation, because third and fourth generations of people *with* Asian roots are born in diaspora, and they do not understand the Asian languages of their grandparents. Losing language is expected as upshot of migration and of invasion. Moreover, holding orientalizing views about Asia is not the privilege just of insensitive foreigners and outsiders. Asian people also hold supremacist views against fellow Asian peoples, and they find support in their rich religious traditions.

---

[6] Gayatri Chakravorty Spivak, *Other Asias* (Malden: Blackwell, 2008), 9–10, 248.

[7] See Roland Boer, "Caught in Between: Australian Biblical Studies between Asia, the Pacific, and the West," in *The Future of the Biblical Past: Envisioning Biblical Studies in a Global Key*, ed. Roland Boer and Fernando F. Segovia (Atlanta: Society of Biblical Literature, 2012), 223–35.

[8] See Kwok Pui-lan, "Finding Ruth a Home: Gender, Sexuality, and the Politics of Otherness," in *Postcolonial Imagination and Feminist Theology* (Louisville: Westminster John Knox, 2005), 100–121.

The caste system deeply ingrained in Hinduism, which divides people and religiously justifies their discriminating against each other,[9] is an example of this. We see similar tendencies in egalitarian religions like Buddhism, as in the case of Sri Lankan Buddhist revivalist Anagarika Dharmapala who favored Sinhalese cultures against his Tamil and Muslim neighbors. Sugirtharajah concludes his evaluation of Dharmapala with a critical observation: "Dharmapala's hermeneutics is a prime example of how natives themselves not only are quite capable of representing themselves but also are equally competent in producing racist, jingoistic, colonialist, nativist, and supremacist theologies."[10]

Asking "Whose Asia?" in a world where borders are holey and migration is ongoing, invites us to respect the complexity of Asian identity and locatedness. We acknowledge three broad Asian locations: First, people in Asian homelands (with their holey borders); second, people in Asian diaspora (on lands that have holey borders as well); third, people returning (remigrants) to Asian homelands. The first generation of Asians in diaspora migrated for a variety of reasons (education, employment, asylum, enslavement, etc.), some at will and some forced, and they have experienced acceptance, rejection, discrimination, and internment[11] in their new homes. In the case of remigrants, some of them "return" when a colonial power departs from their shores (e.g., most recently, when the British "returned" Hong Kong to China), and some return after studying and living in diaspora.[12] These diverse Asians read the bible differently, so any attempt to define biblical criticism in Asia will be an evolving exercise.

---

[9] See e.g., Monica J. Melanchthon, "Unleashing the Power Within: The Bible and Dalits," in *The Future of a Biblical Past: Envisioning Biblical Studies on a Global Key*, ed. Roland Boer and Fernando R. Segovia (Atlanta: Society of Biblical Literature, 2012), 50–52 (49–65).

[10] Sugirtharajah, *Bible and Asia*, 150.

[11] See Johnny Miles, "The 'Enemy Within': Refracting Colonizing Rhetoric in Narratives of Gibeonite and Japanese Identity," in *Postcolonialism and the Hebrew Bible: The Next Step*, ed. Roland Boer (Atlanta: Society of Biblical Literature, 2013), 129–68.

[12] See Yong-Sung Ahn, "For a Better Future in Korean Biblical Studies: Dialoguing within Myself in a Different Context," in *The Future of a Biblical Past: Envisioning Biblical Studies on a Global Key*, ed. Roland Boer and Fernando R. Segovia (Atlanta: Society of Biblical Literature, 2012), 67–79.

Reading in Asia

It is no accident that the itch to define Asian biblical criticism is stronger among Asian scholars in diaspora,[13] who live and read among hyphenated and hybridized peoples, than among Asian scholars at their homelands. Gale A. Yee's experience helps explain the cause of this itch: "Except for my face and name, none of the usual ethnic markers of being Asian fit me, yet white society compels me, however well-intended, to explain how my Asian Americanness makes me different."[14] In diaspora, Asians live in societies that are liminal, diverse and complex, where they are always seen as different. They are Asians; they do not belong in America or in Europe. It thus makes sense, especially for first generation Asian migrants, to want to define what it means to be Asian.

The struggles of Asian remigrants *as* remigrants, on the other hand, have not taken their place in the conversation, for their itch is not the expectation of the white society but the expectation of local peoples in their homelands. They return with foreign accents and western mannerisms, and the locals treat them as if they are westerners (foreigners).[15] As remigrants seek to belong, they take on the responsibility of speaking on behalf of local interests and identities instead of their own experiences *as* remigrants.

A systematic survey of Asian biblical criticism is lacking, and the interaction and interchange between Asian scholars in the homelands (some are homegrown, and some are remigrants) and in diaspora is kindled through joint publications[16] and by the recently formed Society of Asian Biblical Studies (SABS).[17] Our aim in this section is to mark steppingstones for surveyors of Asian biblical criticism, realizing that the

---

[13] See e.g., Mary F. Foskett and Jeffrey Kah-Jin Kuan, eds., *Ways of Being, Ways of Reading: Asian American Biblical Interpretation* (St. Louis: Chalice, 2006) and Tat-siong Benny Liew, *What Is Asian American Biblical Hermeneutics? Reading the New Testament* (Honolulu: University of Hawaii Press, 2008).
[14] Gale A. Yee, "Yin/Yang Is Not Me: An Exploration into an Asian American Biblical Hermeneutics," in *Ways of Being, Ways of Reading: Asian American Biblical Interpretation,* ed. Mary F. Foskett and Jeffrey Kah-Jin Kuan (St. Louis: Chalice, 2006), 153 (152–63).
[15] See Jione Havea, "Would the Real Native Please Sit Down!" in *Faith in a Hyphen: Cross-cultural Theologies Down Under,* ed. Clive Pearson (Parramatta: UTC Publications and Openbook, 2004), 199–210.
[16] Cf. the collection of essays in Foskett and Kuan, *Ways of Being, Ways of Reading*.
[17] The spark for this collection came from the 2012 SABS meeting at Sabah Theological Seminary, Kota Kinabalu, Sabah, Malaysia.

state of Asian biblical criticism cannot be fixed and a survey of it will not be inclusive.

Attending to identity and location (context) is crucial.[18] One Asian reading of the book of Ruth that focuses on these factors is by Angela Wong. Wong uses the lens of history and identity to read the book of Ruth within the context of Asia.[19] Following Andre LaCocque, Wong understands Ruth's place in Israelite society as subversive. Indeed, she argues that ethnic minorities "are needed for the vitality of a dominant culture."[20] Hence, although some scholars view Ruth as a betrayer of her origins, Wong instead presents the positive case for the positive benefits of ethnic minorities within dominant cultures. She draws on the idea of "hybridized" identities to view Ruth's "imagining" herself into Israelite history and identity, instead of asserting her own name, ethnicity, and god. With an eye to the conflicts between aboriginals and new immigrants in many parts of Asia, Wong draws on the work of Anne Pattel-Gray, who explains how Indigenous Australians similarly derive their identity not through asserting their own names but through their spiritual connection to the land in which they live.[21] Since minority groups have much to contribute, Wong calls for an appreciation of these contributions and for a willingness to seek reconciliation within communities.

The contribution by Surekha Nelavala (chapter 7) in this collection draws on her communal context to shed light on an interaction in the book of Ruth. On the background of an Indian household and joint family system, Nelavala suggests that the relationship that forms between Naomi and Ruth is driven by sisterhood and "mutual empathy," rather than by patriarchal or feminist impulses. It is in this way that Ruth is viewed as "a liberationist and a humanist."

Identity and context are important in an Asian biblical approach, but there are other concerns to take into account. We will briefly identify three areas—Asian scriptures, communities, missions—in the wakes of two collections of essays (written in English) rooted in Asian homelands:

---

[18] See R. S. Sugirtharajah, ed., *Voices from the Margins: Reading the Bible in the Third World*, Revised and expanded 3rd ed. (New York: Maryknoll, 2006).
[19] Wai Ching Wong, "Identity in Hybridity: Ruth in the Genealogy of Jesus: Matthew 1:1–17; Ruth 1–4," *Theologies and Cultures* 6 (2009): 98–109.
[20] Wong, "Identity in Hybridity," 102.
[21] Anne Pattel-Gray, *Through Aboriginal Eyes: The Cry from the Wilderness* (Geneva: WCC Publications, 1991).

(1) *Scripture, Community and Mission*,[22] which includes papers presented at a meeting of the Network of Theology Enquiry (NOTE) at Chennai, India in 2002, and (2) *Mapping and Engaging the Bible in Asian Cultures*,[23] which includes papers presented at the biannual meeting of SABS at Seoul, Korea in 2008. While there are publications in Asia's many vernaculars as well as English publications in the Asian diaspora, our decision to focus on these two collections is because they are not well-known among English speaking communities of biblical scholars outside of Asia.[24]

Asian Scriptures

That Asia is polyscriptural has been well-argued, but most Asian biblical critics do not give Asian scriptures the same respect they give Judeo-Christian scriptures.[25] A strong spirit of conservatism elevates Judeo-Christian scriptures above Asian scriptures and Asian cultures, with the latter being treated as means for making sense of the former.[26] This is the setting for Archie C. C. Lee's invitation for *cross-scriptural* reading, which involves reading a biblical text(s) with Asian scriptural text(s). Lee hopes

---

[22] Philip L. Wickeri, ed., *Scripture, Community, and Mission: Essays in Honor of D. Preman Niles* (Hong Kong: Christian Council of Asia; London: Council of World Missions, 2002).

[23] Yeong Mee Lee and Yoon Jong Yoo, eds., *Mapping and Engaging the Bible in Asian Cultures: Congress of the Society of Asian Biblical Studies 2008 Seoul Conference* (Seoul: Christian Literature Society of Korea, 2009).

[24] We acknowledge at the outset that many Asian biblical critics do not showcase their rootedness in their readings. In fact, the nine essays in Part II of *Mapping and Engaging the Bible in Asian Cultures* focus on "contemporary issues" but do not bring those to bear on Asian contexts.

[25] Kwok Pui-lan, "Postcolonialism, Feminism and Biblical Interpretation" in *Scripture, Community, and Mission: Essays in Honor of D. Preman Niles,* ed. Philip L. Wickeri (Hong Kong: Christian Council of Asia; London: Council of World Missions, 2002), 261–62 (261–76).

[26] See e.g., Yim Tesoo, "Interpretation of the Law and the Gospel in Exodus from the Perspective of Minjung Theology," in *Mapping and Engaging the Bible in Asian Cultures: Congress of the Society of Asian Biblical Studies 2008 Seoul Conference,* ed. Yeong Mee Lee and Yoon Jong Yoo (Seoul: Christian Literature Society of Korea, 2009), 93 (89–102); and Wei Huang, "The Meaning of *h'lm* in Qoheleth 3:11 from a Chinese Perspective" in *Mapping and Engaging the Bible in Asian Cultures: Congress of the Society of Asian Biblical Studies 2008 Seoul Conference,* ed. Yeong Mee Lee and Yoon Jong Yoo (Seoul: Christian Literature Society of Korea, 2009), 103 (103–10). Both essays appeal to something Asian to help make sense of something biblical.

that readers may honor Asian scriptures as sacred and significant texts (as they regard biblical texts) rather than as context or illustration for understanding and adopting the biblical text(s).[27]

> Unless we dare to step outside the security and the certainty allegedly promised by dogmatism and absolutism of the one interpretation of "my own scripture," we will be restricted and constrained by the ghetto we established and we will be liable to the inherent hostility created by a certain reduced knowledge of reality.[28]

Cross-scriptural reading requires "inclusive imagination"[29] that celebrates difference and diversity instead of dualistic thinking and colonialist tendencies. Cross-scriptural reading is not syncretistic (for texts change their flavors) or synthetic (for texts lose their flavors) but symbiotic: "a living encounter of the texts within the encounter of religions, resulting in a further articulation of implicit meanings which these texts would not reveal unless they are mutually exposed to each other's illuminating disclosures."[30] Hence it is necessary to cross-check as one reads across scriptures.[31] In this symbiotic experience the cross-scriptural reader can hear the polyphonic voices of the bible. "In the Hebrew Scripture there is a host of different voices embodied in the text, but there are also the unheard voices of the Bible. They are the suppressed voice, the disputed voice, the silenced voice and the little voice."[32]

---

[27] Archie C. C. Lee, "The Bible in Asia: Contesting and Contextualizing" in *Mapping and Engaging the Bible in Asian Cultures: Congress of the Society of Asian Biblical Studies 2008 Seoul Conference*, ed. Yeong Mee Lee and Yoon Jong Yoo (Seoul: Christian Literature Society of Korea, 2009), 23 (19–35).
[28] Ibid., 33.
[29] Cf. Satoko Yamaguchi, "From Dualistic Thinking toward Inclusive Imagination" in *Mapping and Engaging the Bible in Asian Cultures: Congress of the Society of Asian Biblical Studies 2008 Seoul Conference*, ed. Yeong Mee Lee and Yoon Jong Yoo (Seoul: Christian Literature Society of Korea, 2009), 53–71.
[30] Aloysius Pieris, "Cross-Scripture Reading in Buddhist-Christian Dialogue: A Search for the Right Method," in *Scripture, Community, and Mission: Essays in Honor of D. Preman Niles*, ed. Philip L. Wickeri (Hong Kong: Christian Council of Asia; London: Council of World Missions, 2002), 239 (229–50).
[31] Kyung Sook Lee, "Neo-Confucian Ideology in the Interpretation of the Book of Ruth: Toward a Cross-checking Hermeneutics" in *Korean Feminists in Conversation with the Bible, Church and Society*, ed. Kyung Sook Lee and Kyung Mi Park (Sheffield: Sheffield Phoenix, 2011), 1–13.
[32] Archie C. C. Lee, "Polyphonic Voices in the Bible" in *Scripture, Community, and Mission: Essays in Honor of D. Preman Niles*, ed. Philip L. Wickeri (Hong Kong:

In this vein, Mai-Anh Le Tran reads the stories of Lot and Ruth alongside a story from Vietnamese folk tradition.[33] Tô Thị is the name of a young wife who, in Vietnamese cultural songs and poetry, was changed into stone. She stands holding a child in her arms, eternally waiting for her husband. Tran finds that this faithful, selfless character, steadfastly committed to her husband, intersects with the depiction of Ruth. Through her actions, Ruth is given the role of "redeemer" in Israel's salvation history.[34] For Tran, reading the juxtaposed stories raises questions such as, what is "redemption"? What is Ruth saved from? And for what?[35] From a feminist postcolonial perspective, Tran wonders if it was better for Ruth to find home and husband or to be petrified like Lot's wife or Tô Thị.[36]

The contributions by Elaine Goh (chapter 6) and Yan Lin (chapter 4) in this collection are also in step with Lee's invitation. Goh's methodology has some similarities with Tran's, in that Goh reads Ruth intertextually with Prov 31:10–31, within a Malaysian Chinese Christian context. Drawing on Confucian ideals and Malaysian cultural expectations, Goh provides some helpful insights for contemporary women, both in Malaysia and beyond.

Yan Lin's contribution (chapter 4) raises another question: What counts as scripture? The popular position is that scriptures are the sacred texts of established religions. There are, however, stories, legends, and myths that have sacred status in many settings in Asia and beyond, such as the Madurai Veeran Legend[37] and the story of a Pair of Peacocks that

---

Christian Council of Asia; London: Council of World Missions, 2002), 181 (177–92).

[33] Mai-Anh Le Tran, "Lot's Wife, Ruth, and Tô Thị: Gender and Racial Representation in a Theological Feast of Stories" in *Ways of Being, Ways of Reading: Asian American Biblical Interpretation*, ed. Mary F. Foskett and Jeffrey Kah-Jin Kuan (St. Louis: Chalice, 2006), 123–36.

[34] Ibid, 132.

[35] Ibid, 133.

[36] For another reading of Ruth that questions whether Ruth should be viewed as a model for Asian women, see Anna May Say Pa, "Reading Ruth 3:1–5 from an Asian Woman's Perspective," in *Engaging the Bible in a Gendered World: An Introduction to Feminist Biblical Interpretations in Honor of Katherine Doob Sakenfeld*, ed. Linda Day and Carolyn Pressler (Louisville: Westminster John Knox, 2006), 47–59.

[37] See Maria Arul Raja, "Breaking Hegemonic Boundaries: An Intertextual Reading of the Madurai Veeran Legend and Mark's Story of Jesus" in *Scripture, Community, and Mission: Essays in Honor of D. Preman Niles*, ed. Philip L. Wickeri

Yan Lin reads cross-textually with the book of Ruth.[38] Not only is Asia rich with scriptures rooted in religious movements, but Asia is rich with scriptures that are rooted in the memories and lives of people. Should not readers honor those scriptures in the same way that they honor religious scriptures?[39]

Communities

Biblical critics in Asia are not free of communal ties and responsibilities or disengaged from political and societal struggles. Asian biblical critics are conditioned by the religious communities around them, but the (Western) push for academic objectivism often win out and many Asian scholars shy away from naming and engaging their communal roots. On the other hand, scholars who are not so troubled read in conversation with leaders and traditions in their communities.[40] This is not such a radical claim, because readers in Africa and the Americas, Europe and the Caribbean, are also conditioned and affected. No matter where one reads, there is no sterilized reader and no tame context.

What is attractive to us about Asian readers (and we are biased, of course) is the appreciation of being rooted in faith and/or outcast communities. There is no anxiety in belonging to confessing[41] and/or

---

(Hong Kong: Christian Council of Asia; London: Council of World Missions, 2002), 251–60.

[38] Cf. Sugirtharajah's affirmation of Asian fictions and novels in *Bible and Asia*, 224–57.

[39] See similar invitation in Jione Havea, "Engaging scriptures from Oceania" in Jione Havea, David Neville and Elaine Wainwright, eds., *Bible, Borders, Belongings: Engaging readings from Oceania*, Semeia Studies (Atlanta: Society of Biblical Literature, 2014), 3–19.

[40] See Paul Swarup, "The Bible in the Context of Multi-Textual Communities: A Study of Pandita Ramabai's Response (1858–1922)," in *Scripture, Community, and Mission: Essays in Honor of D. Preman Niles*, ed. Philip L. Wickeri (Hong Kong: Christian Council of Asia; London: Council of World Missions, 2002), 204–22; and Francis X. D'Sa, "How Is It That We Hear, Each of Us, in Our Own Native Language? A Tentative Cross-cultural Reading of the Incarnation (John 1) and Avatara (Bhagavadgita 4)," in *Scripture, Community, and Mission: Essays in Honor of D. Preman Niles*, ed. Philip L. Wickeri (Hong Kong: Christian Council of Asia; London: Council of World Missions, 2002), 123–46.

[41] See Tai Il Wang, "Performing the Scripture: Understanding the Bible from Korean Biblical Hermeneutics," in *Mapping and Engaging the Bible in Asian Cultures: Congress of the Society of Asian Biblical Studies 2008 Seoul Conference*, ed. Yeong Mee Lee and Yoon Jong Yoo (Seoul: Christian Literature Society of Korea,

stigmatized communities like the Minjungs[42] and Dalits.[43] Readers can be critical of scriptural texts (qua products of the priestly class, who present their perspectives as Vedic authority) and of their communities (founded on scripturalized discrimination and exclusion), with the awareness that "texts shape communities and their identities and in turn [texts] are shaped by them [communities]."[44] In the intersection of text, interpretation, and community, the challenge is to give voice to the silenced. This is where attending to the subjectivities and interests of outcast and minority/minoritized communities is urgent.[45] "The only way to take a context seriously is to take the plurality of identities that make up that context."[46]

Naveen Rao takes up the interests of the Dalits in his reading of the book of Ruth.[47] Reading Ruth in the time of Ezra-Nehemiah leads Rao to posit that the book critiques Persian-sponsored oppression of marginal communities among the returned exiles, especially widowed women. Ruth is a character who unsettles the order that she joins, so making the

---

2009), 42–45 (37–52); and Oh-Young Kwon, "1 Corinthians 12:12–13: An Ethnic Analysis and Its Evaluation from a Korean-Ethnocentric (*danil minjok*) Christian Context," in *Mapping and Engaging the Bible in Asian Cultures: Congress of the Society of Asian Biblical Studies 2008 Seoul Conference,* ed. Yeong Mee Lee and Yoon Jong Yoo (Seoul: Christian Literature Society of Korea, 2009), 123–39.

[42] See Tesoo, "Interpretation of the Law and the Gospel in Exodus from the Perspective of Minjung Theology," and Kim Yong-Bock, "The Bible among the Minjung of Korea: Kairotic Listening and Reading of the Bible," in *Scripture, Community, and Mission: Essays in Honor of D. Preman Niles,* ed. Philip L. Wickeri (Hong Kong: Christian Council of Asia; London: Council of World Missions, 2002), 70–91.

[43] See Monica Jyotsna Melanchthon, "Dalit Reading of Genesis 10–11:9," in *Scripture, Community, and Mission: Essays in Honor of D. Preman Niles,* ed. Philip L. Wickeri (Hong Kong: Christian Council of Asia; London: Council of World Missions, 2002), 161–76.

[44] Damayanthi M. A. Niles, "Whose Text Is It Anyway? How Text Functions to Build Identity and Community," in *Scripture, Community, and Mission: Essays in Honor of D. Preman Niles,* ed. Philip L. Wickeri (Hong Kong: Christian Council of Asia; London: Council of World Missions, 2002), 313 (304–14).

[45] See also Randall C. Bailey, Tat-siong Benny Liew, and Fernando F. Segovia, eds., *They Were All Together in One Place? Toward Minority Biblical Criticism* (Atlanta: Society of Biblical Literature, 2009).

[46] Niles, "Whose Text Is It Anyway?" 306.

[47] Naveen Rao, "The Book of Ruth as a Clandestine Scripture to Sabotage Persian Colonial Agenda: A Paradigm for a Liberative Dalit Scripture," *Bangalore Theological Forum* 41 (2009): 114–34.

established society "more open to differences and otherness."[48] As a liberative story, Rao finds it to be paradigmatic for the formulation of a liberative scripture by the Dalits in India.

The contribution by Roi Nu (chapter 5) in this collection especially reads from the context of a minority group in Myanmar. Nu compares the Kachin custom of *karat hta ai* with the levirate custom in the Bible in general and the book of Ruth in particular. In light of her comparison, she questions whether we should understand Ruth and Boaz's marriage as following the levirate custom. Nu then draws implications for the Kachin Christians of Myanmar, both female and male.

Seeing that Asia is filled to the brim with people and rhythms, flavors and colors, poverty and riches, hope and despair, industries and philosophies, and so on, objectivism is unacceptable. Moreover, communitarianism is unavoidable. The challenge of this observation is more critical in circles, in Asia and yonder, where detachment and disengagement are favored.

Missions

The Bible came to Asia as the scripture of the Christian mission, one of the partners of Western colonization alongside which it sought to civilize, enlighten, and save Asian (*qua yaxiya-n*) peoples. "During the missionary era, Christian proclamation was essentially a one-way traffic: Christian missions assumed that they possessed the truths necessary for salvation and the people were treated as missiological objects, passive recipients of such pronouncements."[49] It makes sense therefore that there is a strong leaning toward postcolonial criticism among Asian biblical critics.[50] The contributions by Peter Lau (chapter 2) and Sin lung Tong (chapter 3) to this collection come under the umbrella of postcolonial criticism. Lau calls for a reinstatement of the importance of the "world of the text" in postcolonial readings. He illustrates his postcolonial approach by using it to highlight themes in the book of Ruth and then how these themes might have been understood in the time of Ezra-Nehemiah. Tong draws on the postcolonial concept of mimicry to read Ruth's confession (Ruth 1:16–17). He argues that the mimicry found in the Ruth narrative provides space for the marginalized to survive. Tong then applies this concept to the situation in Hong Kong, suggesting that

---

[48] Ibid, 129.
[49] Kwok Pui-lan, "Postcolonialism, Feminism and Biblical Interpretation," 261.
[50] See e.g., R.S. Sugirtharajah, *Asian Biblical Hermeneutics and Postcolonialism: Contesting the Interpretations* (New York: Maryknoll, 1998).

it can be a "source of imagination" for Hong Kong people to reconsider their relationship with China.

The voices and insights that gather in this book exhibit, as a collection, postcolonial tendencies. This is not to say that this collection is *only* postcolonial. Herein also is the mode of reading Sugirtharajah and Kwok call nativist: "The Nativist mode challenges both the Western theories and the elitist Orientalist approach by reviving the vernacular tradition and the use of popular resources."[51]

The supremacist attitudes of the Christian mission are out of place in Asia's multireligious setting, where solidarity and openness are encouraged. For Kwok, this requires reading "the biblical texts in community [especially with other oppressed and stigmatized subjects], so that we can confront our prejudices, and be aware of how our social location influences our reading practices."[52]

One Asian reading of the book of Ruth that considers the multireligious setting is by Hisako Kinukawa. She takes the story of Ruth as an invitation for openness to people of other faiths and cultures.[53] Kinukawa draws parallels between the multireligious Japanese context and that of Moab. She highlights the flexibility of Ruth's faith in committing herself to Naomi's God, which Kinukawa suggests is driven by Ruth's love and commitment to her mother-in-law. In a sense, God is understood to be multireligious: "The confession of Ruth is the evidence of God's endless flexibility and breadth."[54] Hence, Ruth's commitment to Yahweh is viewed not so much as a conversion but as a model for how readers should accept people of other faiths.

Asia of course has Eastern forms of enlightenment and ancient civilizations, with sets of empires established according to their scriptures and missions. These have not yet surfaced on the horizons of Asian biblical criticism, hence a lot more remain to be addressed.

---

[51] Kwok Pui-lan, "Postcolonialism, Feminism and Biblical Interpretation," 265.
[52] Ibid, 273.
[53] Hisako Kinukawa, "'And Your God My God': How We Can Nurture Openness to Other Faiths; Ruth 1:1–19 Read from a Feminist Perspective of a Multi-Faith Community," in *Scripture, Community, and Mission: Essays in Honor of D. Preman Niles,* ed. Philip L. Wickeri (Hong Kong: Christian Council of Asia; London: Council of World Missions, 2002), 193–208.
[54] Ibid, 207.

Postcolonize This

The arrangement of the essays in this collection is somewhat unorthodox or, more appropriately, *yaxiyan*! The survey of strands of reading in the previous section culminates in postcolonial criticism, and the chapters that follow start with the postcolonial readings by Lau and Tong followed by the cross-textual reading by Lin. This collection thus sets out from where Asian biblical criticism is said to be.

The essays by Nu, Goh, and Nelavala follow and, in different ways, are dedicated to reading Ruth from various points in the varied contexts of Asia. What's attractive about centering these three chapters is that, together, they are women-focused and at once community- and family-sensitive. Given that form (and not just content) conditions what this collection *says* and *does*, the centering of these three chapters, in the path of postcolonial reading, invites a rethinking of the politics of identity and of the cons of contextual reading. The attention to identity and context in this collection is not selfish (individualistic) or ethnocentric but familial and communitarian.

Rees and Havea draw this collection to a close by problematizing the limits of Asia and stirring the plot once again. At the end, much to the story of Ruth falls through the gaps of this collection, for other readers from other regions to glean and bring to the threshing floor!

ANOTHER POSTCOLONIAL READING OF THE BOOK OF RUTH[*]

Peter H. W. Lau

At its core, a postcolonial hermeneutic is one of resistance, used to rail against all forms of hegemonic power, including political, social, economic, and ideological. Applied to biblical texts, a postcolonial hermeneutic can be helpful in highlighting and undermining abuses of power. Bradley Crowell notes that, within Hebrew Bible (HB) studies, the current trend is to apply postcolonialism in three ways:

(1) The role of empires and reactions to them in the composition of HB texts.
(2) How colonial empires interpreted the HB and how indigenous populations reacted to colonial interpretations.
(3) Interpretations from previously colonised populations.[1]

Hence, in relation to the biblical text, most postcolonial approaches focus on the world behind or in front of the text.[2] Although a handful of

---

[*] Sections of this chapter are modified from Peter H. W. Lau, *Identity and Ethics in the Book of Ruth: A Social Identity Approach*, BZAW 416 (Berlin: de Gruyter, 2011), and an earlier version of this chapter was presented at the 2011 SBL International Meeting in London. I would like to thank the participants of the session for their feedback and to Mark Brett for comments on an earlier draft.

[1] Bradley L. Crowell, "Postcolonial Studies and the Hebrew Bible," *Currents in Biblical Research* 7 (2009): 217–44.

[2] The world behind the text considers the historical, social and cultural backgrounds in which a text was written, and which might have motivated its composition. The world of the text considers the events and characters of the text to discern what response the implied author might have desired from an implied reader. The world in front of the text considers the application of a text to real readers, and the interplay between the text and readers in particular historico-social contexts. W. Randolph Tate, *Biblical Interpretation: An Integrated Approach*, 3rd edition (Peabody: Hendrickson, 2008), 2–4, summarises these as author-centered, text-centered, and reader-centered, respectively.

postcolonial studies have been sensitive to the world of the text,[3] by and large there has been a relative neglect of this aspect of the text.

Some practitioners of postcolonial biblical criticism may challenge even the necessity of this tripartite division. For instance, R. S. Sugirtharajah avers that, from a colonial perspective, Western biblical scholarship, with its reference to author-centered, text-centered, and reader-centered hermeneutics, is transcended by a simpler distinction: colonial and postcolonial.[4] Yet other practitioners of postcolonial biblical criticism are more explicit in describing their approach to the Bible. Fernando Segovia, for example, asserts:

> I would eschew any type of formulation that would imply or suggest ... the presence of ... stable meaning in the text, ... or *the world of the text*— formulations along the lines of ... letting the text speak, ... or achieving a fuller meaning of the text.[5]

Since both Sugirtharajah and Segovia have been influential in postcolonial biblical studies, this would explain, at least in part, why there has been a neglect of the world of the text.

But from the perspective of biblical studies, the world of the text is an essential aspect of interpretation. Anthony Thiselton argues that the processes within the three worlds should be explored as complementary tasks.[6] Similarly, Randolph Tate warns that meaning is impaired when one or more worlds are neglected.[7] Naturally, different hermeneutical

---

[3] E.g., Mark G. Brett, *Decolonizing God: The Bible in the Tides of Empire* (Sheffield: Sheffield Phoenix, 2008); Philip Chia, "On Naming the Subject: Postcolonial Reading of Daniel 1," *Jian Dao* 7 (1997): 17–36; Daniel C. Timmer, "The Intertextual Jonah face à l'empire: The Post-colonial Significance of the Book's Cotexts and Purported Neo-Assyrian Context," *JHS* 9 (2009): 1–22. Cf. David A. DeSilva, "Using the Master's Tools to Shore Up Another's House: A Postcolonial Analysis of 4 Maccabees," *JBL* 126 (2007): 99–127.
[4] R. S. Sugirtharajah, "Biblical Studies after the Empire: From a Colonial to a Postcolonial Mode of Interpretation," in *The Postcolonial Bible*, ed. R. S. Sugirtharajah (Sheffield: Sheffield Academic Press, 1998), 15.
[5] Fernando F. Segovia, in *Teaching The Bible: The Discourses and Politics of Biblical Pedagogy*, ed. Fernando F. Segovia and Mary Ann Tolbert (Maryknoll: Orbis, 1998), 140 (emphasis added).
[6] Cf. Anthony C. Thiselton, "'Behind' and 'In Front of' the Text: Language, Reference and Indeterminancy" in *After Pentecost: Language and Biblical interpretation*, ed. Craig Bartholomew, Colin Greene, and Karl Möller, Scripture and Hermeneutics 2 (Carlisle: Paternoster, 2001), 116.
[7] Tate, *Biblical Interpretation*, 5–7.

approaches will highlight one or more worlds; nonetheless, all three worlds need to at least be considered to produce a polychromatic reading.

This chapter thus considers the three worlds, but since the world of the text is relatively neglected, it will especially focus on this world in order to demonstrate its fruitfulness within a postcolonial hermeneutic.

The first part of this chapter adopts a postcolonial approach to reading the Ruth narrative (RN). Intertextuality[8] and identity[9] are prominent elements of the postcolonial approach and will be used to explore what ideologies or powers the world of the RN might be resisting. The intertexts that will be brought into dialogue with the RN are those HB texts explicitly referred to in the RN and other canonical texts that shed light on the RN. Since the intertextual connections of Ruth have been explored extensively elsewhere,[10] this chapter will focus on the intertexts that modify or reinforce the identities of the main characters.

The second part of this chapter applies the observations of the first to the Persian Period. Core elements of Israelite identity in the early Restoration period will be explored and how these aspects of identity might be resisted or reinforced by the Ruth narrative.

---

[8] Postcolonial studies are receptive to the interaction that various "texts" have with one another, both written and non-written.

[9] "The question of identity traverses post-colonial thinking"; Peter Childs, Jean Jacques Weber, and Patrick Williams, *Post-Colonial Theory and Literatures: African, Caribbean and South Asian* (Trier: Wissenschaftlicher Verlag Trier, 2006), 13.

[10] See, e.g., James Black, "Ruth in the Dark: Folktale, Law and Creative Ambiguity in the Old Testament," *Literature and Theology* 5 (1991): 20–36; Georg Braulik, "The Book of Ruth as Intra-Biblical Critique of the Deuteronomic Law," *AcT* 19 (1999): 1–20; Michael D. Goulder, "Ruth: A Homily on Deuteronomy 22–25?" in *Of Prophets, Visions and Wisdom of Sages: Essays in Honour of R. Norman Whybray on his Seventieth Birthday,* ed. Heather A. McKay and David J. A. Clines, JSOTSup 162 (Sheffield: Almond, 1993), 307–19; André LaCocque, *Ruth,* trans. K. C. Hanson (Minneapolis: Fortress, 2004); Kirsten Nielsen, *Ruth: A Commentary,* trans. Edward Broadbridge (Louisville: Westminster John Knox, 1997); Ellen van Wolde, "Texts in Dialogue with Texts: Intertextuality in the Ruth and Tamar Narratives," *BibInt* 5 (1997): 1–27; Yair Zakovitch, *Das Buch Rut: Ein jüdischer Kommentar,* trans. Andreas Lehnardt, SBS 177 (Stuttgart: Katholisches Bibelwerk, 1999).

Israelite Identity

In this chapter, I maintain that the dominant notion of Israelite identity is challenged by the Ruth text. In the world of the Ruth text, Israelite identity is primarily defined by a right relationship with YHWH, as expressed in acts of *ḥesed*—which often involves sacrifice and risk.[11] This will be demonstrated through an examination of four characters: Boaz, Naomi, Ruth and YHWH.

Boaz

In the RN, Boaz is presented as the prototypical Israelite, "a man of great worth" (Ruth 2:1; איש גבור חיל). His vibrant relationship with YHWH is expressed both in word and action. His first words indicate a personal experience of God's blessing and his desire that others enjoy the same: "YHWH be with you!" (Ruth 2:4; יהוה עמכם). Taken alone, this may be understood as just a habitual greeting or an outward show of religiosity.[12] But the genuineness of his faith is seen in his prayer that YHWH would reward Ruth for her *ḥesed* (Ruth 2:12), and especially by his generous actions to Ruth, beyond the requirements of the Law. Intertexts further highlight the quality of Boaz's character and the extent of his *ḥesed*.

In chapter two Boaz provides Ruth with more gleanings than are required in the gleaning law. The number of times this special provision is reinforced in the law suggests it was only reluctantly, if at all, followed by Israelite landowners (Exod 22:22–24; Lev 19:9–10; 23:22; Deut 10:18; 14:29; 16:11; 24:19–21). And the exhortations of the Prophets indicate that this was an ongoing, ingrained problem (e.g., Isa 1:21–23; 10:1–2; Amos 5:11–15; 8:4–6; Mic 3:1–3; cf. Job 24:4, 21; Ps 94:6). Yet not only does Boaz seem to delight in following the gleaning law, he goes beyond its specific requirements (Ruth 2:8–9, 10, 14, 15–16, 18). In this light, Boaz's generosity is all the more remarkable; his act of *ḥesed* is over against the norm of his society.

---

[11] It is difficult to find a single English equivalent to *ḥesed* (חסד). Translations emphasizing obligation are inappropriate; e.g., *HALOT* 1:336–37. Those translations emphasizing goodness or kindness capture the sense better; e.g., BDB, 338–39. While "loving-kindness" is probably the closest approximation, I will continue to use *ḥesed* in lieu of an English equivalent.

[12] Cf. Danna N. Fewell and David M. Gunn, "Boaz, Pillar of Society: Measures of Worth in the Book of Ruth," *JSOT* 45 (1989): 46.

In chapter three Boaz does not take advantage of Ruth on the threshing floor, despite the immense temptation he would have felt. While some argue that sexual intercourse did in fact take place,[13] linguistic[14] and narratological[15] evidence points to Boaz and Ruth's continued sexual purity; the literary devices function to evoke the sexual tension and temptation felt by the characters.[16] Boaz overcomes the sexual temptation on the threshing floor and thus emerges as "the antithesis of the lawless characters" common to the historical period of the narrative.[17] Intertexts augment the virtue of Boaz's character: Moabite women are portrayed stereotypically as morally lax (Num 25:1–3); and the story of Lot's incest with his daughters spells out the alternative consequence of a nocturnal visit by a single female to a senior male whose judgment may be impaired by wine (Gen 19:30–38; cf. Ruth 3:7). Boaz's ability to overcome the temptation thus reinforces his singular standing as "a man of great worth" (2:1).

Boaz's actions in chapter four epitomize his *ḥesed* and the accompanying risk and sacrifice involved. The main risk Boaz takes is marrying Ruth. As highlighted by contrast with the nearer kinsman, in redeeming the field and marrying Ruth, Boaz risked jeopardizing his own estate (Ruth 4:6). Furthermore, he also risked his reputation by marrying a foreigner, an action forbidden by some sections of the Law (cf. Deut 7:1–4; 23:3–6). And if he were single there is also a risk to his own family line if Ruth were subfertile.[18] After all, Ruth was married for

---

[13] E.g., Calum M. Carmichael, "'Treading' in the Book of Ruth," *ZAW* 92 (1980): 257; Anthony Phillips, "The Book of Ruth: Deception and Shame," *JJS* 37 (1986): 14.

[14] The phrasing of Boaz's request for Ruth to "remain tonight" (ליני הלילה; Ruth 3:13; cf. 1:16) rather than "lie down" (שכב), is devoid of any sexual undertone. Cf. Edward F. Campbell, *Ruth*, AB 7 (Garden City: Doubleday, 1975), 137–38; Zakovitch, *Rut*, 144.

[15] Chapter 4 would be superfluous if the marriage was already consummated in chapter 3. The description, "So Boaz took Ruth, and she became his wife. And he went to her" (Ruth 4:13), would be out of order. See Ellen van Wolde, *Ruth and Naomi* (London: SCM, 1997), 84–85.

[16] Moshe J. Bernstein, "Two Multivalent Readings in the Ruth Narrative," *JSOT* 50 (1991): 17–20.

[17] Harry J. Harm, "The Function of Double Entendre in Ruth Three," *JOTT* 7 (1995): 23; Schadrac Keita and Janet W. Dyk, "The Scene at the Threshing Floor: Suggestive Readings and Intercultural Considerations on Ruth 3," *BT* 57 (2006): 17–32.

[18] The case for Boaz's bachelor status is presented in Lau, *Identity and Ethics*, 76–83.

up to ten years without producing a child. If she were only ever able to bear one son, this son—by being attributed to Ruth's deceased husband Mahlon—would continue Elimelech's, not Boaz's line. Intertexts further enhance the virtue of Boaz's character by revealing that there was no legal obligation for Boaz to redeem the land and marry Ruth: he was not the nearest kinsman, and he was not a brother-in-law (Lev 25:23–25; Deut 25:5–10). In fact, Gen 38 reveals that the levirate responsibility was often considered an onerous task. But driven by *ḥesed*, and at great personal cost, Boaz was willing to take the risk.[19] Along with the nearer kinsman's response, the intertexts reveal Boaz's attitude as one of resistance to the societal norm. That he is memorialized in Israelite history as an ancestor of king David, while the nearer kinsman is left anonymous, only serves to underscore the importance of *ḥesed* as a core component of Israelite identity.

Taken as a whole, Boaz's actions also resist a restrictive application of the law. In relation to the gleaning, redemption and levirate laws, close adherence to their specific requirements is eschewed for expansive application. This is consistent with the narrative application of the levirate law in Gen 38, where only two of the three requirements for a levirate union are fulfilled.[20] It is also consistent with an understanding of the redemption law within its broader context: "brother" (אח) not only denotes a male sibling with the same parent(s), but also a clansman from the wider kinship group.[21] In short, Boaz's actions broaden the scope of the law by acting consistently with the moral principle underlying the law. Or, in other words, Boaz applies the law according to the principle of *ḥesed*.

---

[19] Boaz not only pays for the field, he must also pay for the upkeep of Naomi and Ruth. After fathering a son, he must provide for him also. As Charles Halton, "An Indecent Proposal: The Theological Core of the Book of Ruth," *SJOT* 26 (2012): 39, aptly notes, *ḥesed* is "being willing to take extreme measures for the sake of others."

[20] Onan is a brother from the same parents, and his brother Er dies without siring an heir. But the brothers were not living together on an undivided estate after the death of their father, since Judah is still alive.

[21] The clansmen responsible for the redemption of person (Lev 25:48–49) are most likely the same group that is responsible for redemption of land. Cf. Gregory C. Chirichigno, *Debt-Slavery in Israel and the Ancient Near East*, JSOTSup 141 (Sheffield: JSOT Press, 1993), 325; Jacob Milgrom, *Leviticus 23–27*, AB 3B (New York: Doubleday, 2000), 2194.

Naomi

Juxtaposed with Boaz, Naomi is a flawed Israelite; nonetheless, the development of Naomi's character reinforces the core components of Israelite identity. At the outset she leaves Israel's covenant land with her family to seek refuge in a foreign land. While scholars debate the wisdom of the sojourn,[22] the RN and biblical intertexts cast this decision, and hence Naomi's character, in a negative light. For if YHWH "visits" (פקד) Israel to break the famine (1:6), the presumption is that God also allowed the famine. Moreover, many intertexts present famine as punishment for Israel's disobedience (e.g., Lev 26:19–29; Deut 28:23–24, 38–42; 2 Sam 21:1–14; 1 Kgs 17:1; 18:1–2). If this is the case, intertexts suggest that the correct response would have been to repent (e.g., Amos 4:6–9) instead of seeking refuge in a foreign land. Yet Naomi and her family sought refuge in Moab, a choice of location that is also highly questionable. Although it was a neighboring land, it was a country with which Israel intermittently experienced hostile relations, as attested in intertexts (Num 22–25; 1 Sam 14:47; 2 Sam 8:2; 2 Kgs 3:4–27; Isa 15–16; Jer 48; Ezek 25:8–11; Amos 2:1–3; Ezra 9:1; Neh 13:1; cf. Mesha Stele). Pertinently, during the time of the Judges, in which the RN is broadly set, Moab was viewed as an enemy (Judg 3:12–30; 10:6).

Although Elimelech is portrayed as actively leading his family out of Israel, there is a hint in the world of the text that Naomi was also involved in the decision. As the chapter opens, Elimelech is the subject of the verbs as the one who leaves Bethlehem to sojourn in Moab (Ruth 1:1–2a). His wife and family's participation seem a secondary issue (Ruth 1:2b).[23] Yet by the end of the chapter, when Naomi returns to Bethlehem she states, "*I* went away" (אני הלכתי; Ruth 1:21), not "*we* went away." Here Naomi claims some initiative and responsibility for the decision to leave Israel;[24] it was not purely a unilateral decision. Intertexts also support a wife's influence in decision-making. Many examples can be adduced, including Eve (Gen 3:6), Rebekah (Gen 27:46–28:5), Samson's

---

[22] E.g., Frederic W. Bush, *Ruth, Esther,* WBC 9 (Dallas: Word Books, 1996), 67.
[23] Intertextual links with Abraham reinforce this interpretation of male initiative (Gen 12:10): announcements of the famine are identical in both accounts (ויהי רעב בארץ); the references to departure are similar (וילך in Ruth 1:1; וירד in Gen 12:10); and the purpose for leaving is identical (לגור). See Daniel I. Block, *Judges, Ruth,* NAC 6 (Nashville: Broadman & Holman, 1999), 625–26; Nielsen, *Ruth,* 40–41.
[24] Cf. Barry G. Webb, *Five Festal Garments,* NSBT 10 (Leicester: Apollos, 2000), 42; Zakovitch, *Rut,* 103.

wife (Judg 14:15–20), Bathsheba (1 Kgs 1:11–31), and Job's wife (Job 2:9–10).

But whatever Naomi's role was in the decision to leave Israel, we find that her situation improves markedly when she decides to return to Israel. "Return" (שוב) is one of the *Leitworter* in chapter one, occurring twelve times (Ruth 1:6, 7, 8, 10, 11, 12, 15 [twice], 16, 21, 22 [twice]). The use of the word at the beginning and end of the chapter forms an *inclusio*, completing the journey motif, but not only in a geographical sense. The upturn in her situation could be viewed as coincidental. But intertexts point to departure from and return to the land as more than just a physical departure. When Moses foresees Israel's disobedience leading to their expulsion, he also foresees their restoration, but only after Israel returns to YHWH or repents (שוב; Deut 30:1–5).[25] "Return" is also regularly used by the Prophets for repentance. In an intertext that particularly resonates with the RN, Amos indicts Israel for not repenting (שוב), despite YHWH sending famine, pestilence and the sword (Amos 4:6–11). Amos specifically states that YHWH deliberately withheld rain in Israelite towns to induce Israel to repent, but they did not (Ruth 4:7–8). These intertexts suggest that Naomi's return is not only physical, it is also a repentance from sin, a turning back to, and an acknowledgement of trust in YHWH. It was a return to YHWH's sphere of blessing.

From a postcolonial perspective, Naomi functions to resist the notion that genealogy is the only pertinent component of Israelite identity. The portrayal of Naomi turning her back on YHWH and her subsequent suffering, then her restoration to fullness only after repentance displays the importance of a right relationship with YHWH. Thus, within the world of the text Naomi reinforces the importance of a right relationship with YHWH as an essential component of Israelite identity.

Ruth

As a foreigner who is finally accepted into Israelite society, Ruth both reinforces and resists the prevailing understanding of Israelite identity. Ruth's transformation from Moabite to Israelite reinforces Israelite identity. The first step in her transformation is her vow of devotion to the inseparable complex of Naomi, her God, and her people (Ruth 1:16–17).

---

[25] The initiative, however, lies with YHWH, who enables repentance through a circumcision of the heart (Deut 30:6); see Paul A. Barker, *The Triumph of Grace in Deuteronomy: Faithless Israel, Faithful Yahweh in Deuteronomy* (Carlisle: Paternoster, 2004), 163–68.

Yet central to Ruth's vow is her commitment to YHWH, Israel's deity.[26] In contradistinction to Orpah, she has turned from following a number of gods (Ruth 1:15) to exclusive devotion to YHWH. Further evidence of Ruth's allegiance to Israel's deity is found in her appeal that YHWH (יהוה) curse her should she renege, instead of the more general "God" (Ruth 1:17; אלהים). In the world of the text, it is significant that Boaz recognizes Ruth as having resituated herself under YHWH's wings (Ruth 2:12).

The veracity of her change of allegiance is confirmed by her acts of ḥesed, an ethical ideal of her new religion. Non-Israelites also perform ḥesed (Ruth 1:8), but in the world of the text it is an especial characteristic of the people of YHWH. Boaz highlights two of Ruth's actions in particular. He describes Ruth's first act of ḥesed as her abandonment of her homeland and family (Ruth 2:11). Sacrificing the security of her mother's home, she risks everything by committing herself to Naomi. Ruth's second act of ḥesed is, according to Boaz, greater than her first: her choice of him as a marriage partner. In selecting Boaz she displays ḥesed by choosing loyalty to Naomi and her family instead of personal gain. For, by selecting Boaz, a kinsman-redeemer, there is the chance that her father-in-law's field will be redeemed, and his family line will be perpetuated (Ruth 3:12–13).

Yet Ruth's second act of ḥesed also involved risk. As reinforced by intertexts, Naomi's threshing floor scheme, which Ruth agrees to enact, is riddled with danger.[27] As a single woman sent in the dark of night beyond the protection of the city wall, she was at risk of physical assault (Song 5:7). Since threshing floors were associated with prostitution, she was at risk of sexual assault (Hos 9:1). And her reputation was at risk if Boaz misinterpreted her presence at the threshing floor as an attempt at seduction or entrapment, instead of signaling her availability and intention for marriage.

The outcome of Ruth's ḥesed underscores the centrality of this virtue for Israelite identity. As Boaz's wife, she is publicly and concretely bound to Israelite society (Ruth 4:10, 13). Boaz's description of her as "a woman of worth" (Ruth 3:11; אשת חיל) ranks her worthiness as comparable to his own (cf. Ruth 2:1; אש גבור חיל). Boaz's mention of a gate and a worthy woman recalls Prov 31:10–31, an intertext that reinforces

---

[26] Ruth's speech (1:16–17) is symmetrical in structure, with her fealty to YHWH located centrally, highlighting its importance; see Murray D. Gow, *The Book of Ruth: Its Structure, Theme and Purpose* (Leicester: Apollos, 1992), 36–37.

[27] Halton, "An Indecent Proposal," 39, considers Ruth's acquiescence to Naomi's plan as Ruth's most striking demonstration of ḥesed.

Ruth as a virtuous, ideal wife, and paints a picture of her actions as "a woman of worth."[28] The birth of Obed renders her as a valuable contributor to the House of Israel (Ruth 4:11). Ultimately, Ruth's *ḥesed* pays great dividends: she becomes the great-grandmother of the greatest Israelite king (Ruth 4:11, 17–22).

Intertexts further underscore the worthiness of Ruth's membership into Israel. Her decision to leave her native country can be viewed as parallel to the journey undertaken by Abram (Gen 12:1–9); indeed, Ruth's action may be evidence of even greater faith than the Israelite patriarch.[29] Furthermore, although she may be descended from Lot (Gen 19:30–38), she distances herself from her ancestry by not behaving like Lot's eldest daughter on the threshing floor.[30] At the end of the RN Ruth is linked with the patriarchal mothers Rachel and Leah (Ruth 4:11; Gen 29–30)—she now stands in continuity with that line.[31] She is also compared with Tamar (Ruth 4:12; Gen 38), but presented as more virtuous: Tamar resorts to deception, Ruth openly reveals her identity (Ruth 3:9);[32] Tamar is compelled into sexual relations, Ruth maintains her sexual purity.[33]

Hence, Ruth reinforces Israelite identity. Like Naomi, Ruth demonstrates the centrality of turning to YHWH; that is, the importance of a right relationship with YHWH as an essential aspect of Israelite identity. Like Boaz, Ruth demonstrates the importance of a life of *ḥesed* towards others as a core component of Israelite identity, which flows from a right relationship with YHWH. That Ruth is a foreigner serves to distil these two essential components of identity; she reveals that genealogy is not central to Israelite identity.

Yet Ruth's foreignness resists a dominant notion of Israelite identity, viz. that membership is based on genealogical descent. For although she takes on core elements of Israelite identity, she cannot remove all vestiges of her foreignness. Despite Ruth's best efforts to assimilate into

---

[28] The position of the book of Ruth in some Hebrew canons, after Proverbs, is more suggestive of this link. See also chapter by Elaine W. F. Goh in this volume.
[29] Abram left his native land with a trust in God's promise, whereas Ruth left without any promise from God regarding her future; so, e.g., LaCocque, *Ruth*, 53.
[30] Cf. Nielsen, *Ruth*, 68; Zakovitch, *Rut*, 51. For correspondences between the RN and Gen 19:30–38, see Zakovitch, *Rut*, 49–51.
[31] Robert L. Hubbard, *The Book of Ruth*, NICOT (Grand Rapids: Eerdmans, 1988), 259.
[32] Cf. LaCocque, *Ruth*, 92.
[33] For further correspondences between the RN and Gen 38, see Zakovitch, *Rut*, 52–54.

Israelite society and even the public recognition of her change in status to an Israelite (Ruth 4:11–12),³⁴ she would still maintain elements of her Moabite origin. For instance, her complexion or physical attributes may distinguish her immediately, then her mannerisms and use of the Hebrew language (e.g., pronunciation and grammar)³⁵ would betray her Moabite origin. Even with maximal cultural adaptation, she can never completely assimilate into Israelite society.

The repetition of "the Moabitess" (המואביה) in the narrative indicates her status as an "other." This title is mostly found upon her first interaction with Israelite society (Ruth 1:22; 2:1, 6, 21). Yet Boaz's continued use of this designation in the last chapter suggests an element of her foreignness remained, even upon her integration into Israelite society (Ruth 4:5, 10). Although the last two references to Ruth are simply "Ruth" or Naomi's "daughter-in-law" (Ruth 4:13, 15), the double use of "the Moabitess" earlier in the chapter indicates some ambivalence towards her final identity.³⁶ As Adele Berlin observes, there remains an underlying tension "between foreignness and familiarity."³⁷

Or in postcolonial terms she is a hybrid identity,³⁸ neither Moabite nor Israelite, but with elements of both. In relation to identity, hybridity describes the intermingling of identities between colonizer and colonized, which undermines and destabilizes the status quo of the colonizers.³⁹ Hence, Ruth is not only influenced by her host culture; she also influences her host culture. Primarily, her presence raises questions about the essence of Israelite identity. Ruth's presence opposes the idea that Israelite identity is based solely on ethnicity or descent. A foreigner

---

³⁴ Neil Glover, "Your People, My People: An Exploration of Ethnicity in Ruth," *JSOT* 33 (2009): 302.
³⁵ Ironically, Ruth's speech does not display any linguistic particularities, in contrast to the speeches of the native Hebrew speakers Boaz and Naomi. Cf. Campbell, *Ruth*, 25.
³⁶ For further on Ruth's assimilation into Israelite society, see Lau, *Identity and Ethics*, 113–14.
³⁷ Adele Berlin, *Poetics and Interpretation of Biblical Narrative* (Sheffield: Almond Press, 1983), 88.
³⁸ Although a disputed term in postcolonial studies, hybridity commonly refers to "the creation of new transcultural forms within the contact zone created by colonisation." Bill Ashcroft, Gareth Griffiths, and Helen Tiffin, *Post-Colonial Studies: The Key Concepts,* 2nd edition (London: Routledge, 2007), 108.
³⁹ Thomas B. Dozeman, *Methods for Exodus* (Cambridge: Cambridge University Press, 2010), 237.

who turns to YHWH and who lives out a life of *ḥesed* can be valued as an important member of Israel (Ruth 4:11, 17–22).

YHWH

In the world of the text YHWH is identified primarily as the universally sovereign protector and provider. Yet the importance of YHWH as a character is inversely proportional to YHWH's number of appearances: YHWH's intervention is mentioned only twice but YHWH's providence can be understood to traverse the whole narrative. In the first chapter Naomi hears that YHWH has broken the famine in Israel (Ruth 1:6). Although this is hearsay, intertexts support the statement's veracity based on the construction of the phrase[40] and the association of פקד (visit) with YHWH's direct action.[41] Then in the last chapter YHWH grants conception to Ruth (Ruth 4:13). These two interventions bookend and underscore YHWH's providence.[42] Yet although there are no other overt narrative statements of YHWH's action, evidence can be found that YHWH's guiding hand was in all events of the RN.

In chapter one Naomi twice laments that YHWH directly brought calamity upon her (Ruth 1:13, 21). The beginning of chapter two sets up Boaz as a potential benefactor, then Ruth "just happens to end up (ויקר מקרה) in the portion of field belonging to Boaz" (Ruth 2:3). From Ruth's perspective this event may seem coincidental but the event's juxtaposition with the earlier narratorial introduction of Boaz (Ruth 2:1) points to God's providence. This understanding is reinforced by intertexts.[43] The same combination of מקרה ("chance"/"fate") and קרה ("happen"/"befall") occurs in Eccl 2:14, where it is stated that "fate" is beyond the control of humanity. Another intertext is the narrative of Abraham sending his servant to find a wife for Isaac (Gen 24:12–27), in which the servant prays that God would grant him success (קרה) in his task. As the servant afterwards thanks YHWH for fulfilling his request, it is clear that God superintends the outcome (Gen 24:26–27).

---

[40] Intertexts in which characters act after hearing reliable information include Gen 43:25 and 1 Kgs 5:15; Zakovitch, *Rut*, 83.
[41] YHWH "visiting" the people can be in a positive ("to come to aid of;" e.g., Gen 50:24; Exod 4:31; 1 Sam 2:21) or negative ("to punish," e.g., Exod 20:5; Num 14:18; Deut 5:9–10) sense; see BDB, 824–25.
[42] Cf. Campbell, *Ruth*, 69.
[43] Cf. Nielsen, *Ruth*, 55.

As Murray Gow points out, prayers offered in the RN similarly highlight God's providence.[44] Naomi prays for a husband for Orpah and Ruth (Ruth 1:8–9); Boaz prays for YHWH to reward Ruth for her loyalty to Naomi (Ruth 2:11–12); Naomi prays for YHWH's blessing on Boaz (Ruth 2:20); Boaz asks for YHWH's blessing on Ruth for seeking him as a redeemer (Ruth 3:10); the throng at the town gate pray for fertility and prosperity for Ruth and Boaz (Ruth 4:11–12); the women of the town bless YHWH for providing a redeemer and pray that Obed's name be perpetuated (Ruth 4:14–15).[45] These prayers culminate in the marriage of Boaz and Ruth, and YHWH's provision of Obed. The prayers thus point to YHWH's behind-the-scenes control of the whole narrative. The historical backdrop of the RN, the period of the Judges, point to an acknowledgement of YHWH's powerful intervening acts. Yet the RN also reveals another side to YHWH's mode of action: quiet and continuous, working in and through the day-to-day lives of families in ancient Israel.

Underlying the prayers is the concept of retribution: YHWH repays people for their actions—both good and bad. The world of the RN presents YHWH as sovereignly judging the actions of all people. As noted above, YHWH's judgment can be seen at the outset of the narrative, after Elimelech and his family leaves Israel to seek food and protection in a foreign land, Moab. While in a foreign land, Elimelech and his sons meet their demise. Scholars debate whether their deaths can be attributed to YHWH. Certainly, causation is not explicit in the narrative; but at least one intertext suggests that the deaths could be punishment for intermarriage with idolaters (Deut 7:3–4). Naomi, however, shows no hesitation in attributing the misfortune to YHWH (1:13, 20, 21). And when she laments the disaster that God has brought upon her, she uses the name "the Almighty" (שדי; Ruth 1:20, 21). This divine name is pertinent because of its connotation of a sovereign king who brings both blessing and curse.[46] It is the characteristic name of God in Job,[47] an intertext that portrays the suffering of another under the

---

[44] Murray D. Gow, "Ruth," in *New Dictionary of Biblical Theology*, ed. T. Desmond Alexander and Brian S. Rosner (Leicester: InterVarsity, 2000), 176–78.
[45] On blessings functioning as prayers, see Patrick D. Miller, *They Cried to the Lord: The Form and Theology of Biblical Prayer* (Minneapolis: Fortress, 1994), 290–93.
[46] See Tryggve N. D. Mettinger, *In Search of God: The Meaning and Message of the Everlasting Names*, trans. Frederick H. Cryer (Philadelphia: Fortress, 1988), 69–72.
[47] שדי occurs thirty-one times in Job.

hand of "the Almighty."[48] Particularly relevant to this discussion is that God's dominion extends beyond Israel—to the land of Uz.[49]

YHWH not only sovereignly extends his hand in punishment, but he also opens his hand in blessing. The historical backdrop of the RN especially highlights God's *ḥesed* to the people. The general picture of the time of the judges is a period of moral, religious and political chaos, a time of downward-spiraling rebellion against YHWH. Yet despite Israel's persistent rebellion, YHWH still displays *ḥesed* on a national level by rescuing the people through judges, and on a family level by redeeming Naomi and Elimelech's line through Obed and Boaz. YHWH also sovereignly bestows divine blessings internationally. While in Moab, Naomi prays that YHWH would show *ḥesed* to her daughters-in-law and provide husbands for them (Ruth 1:8–9). YHWH's *ḥesed* is thus available beyond the borders of Israel. This expansive understanding of YHWH's *ḥesed* is echoed in Psalm 36:8(7), "How precious is your *ḥesed* [חסד], O God! All people take refuge in the shadow of your wings." The interplay between YHWH's sovereignty in blessing and the role of humankind centers on finding refuge under YHWH's wings. Boaz prays that God would bless Ruth because she had found refuge under YHWH's wings (Ruth 2:12; כנף). Ruth then requests shelter under Boaz's "wing(s)" (Ruth 3:9; כנף),[50] and it finally transpires that YHWH fulfils Boaz's prayer through Boaz himself, for it is through Boaz that YHWH will display his *ḥesed* to Elimelech and his family.

Ruth's change of allegiance, a Moabite joining the Israelite community, further reinforces YHWH's concern for the whole world. This motif resonates with other Hebrew Bible intertexts. The book of Jonah is another short narrative emphasizing YHWH's universal perspective.[51] YHWH's unannounced all-causality is echoed in the book of Esther, where YHWH once again exerts control in a foreign land, among foreign people. And finally, the Patriarchal narratives, which

---

[48] In contrast to Naomi, however, Job is presented as innocent (Job 1:1). As noted above, Naomi was probably involved in the decision to leave Israel.

[49] The exact location of Uz is debated, but it was likely located somewhere from Aram to Edom. Cf. Lamentations 4:21. For further discussion, see David J. A. Clines, *Job 1–20*, WBC (Waco, TX: Word, 1989), 10.

[50] That is, edge of Boaz's garment. כנף could be either singular or dual (as in Ruth 2:12). The singular is used elsewhere in relation to a request for marriage (e.g., Deut 27:20; Ezek 16:8; Mal 2:16), and so is more likely here in the context of Ruth's marriage proposal.

[51] For a recent treatment of this topic see Daniel C. Timmer, *A Gracious and Compassionate God: Mission, Salvation and Spirituality in the Book of Jonah*, NSBT (Nottingham: Apollos, 2011).

have a closer intertextual connection with Ruth, present YHWH's international concern (Gen 12:3) and providential control beyond Israel: for instance, calling Abraham in Haran (Gen 11:31–12:1) and directing Joseph's life, even to Egypt, for the ultimate benefit of both Israelite and foreigner (Gen 50:20).

This presentation of YHWH as the universally sovereign deity motivates Israelites and non-Israelites alike to trust in YHWH and display *ḥesed* in their own lives, because YHWH is their provider and protector. All people can freely show *ḥesed* to others, because they can rely on YHWH, the ultimate source of *ḥesed*. Indeed, by living this way, they reflect the character of YHWH, from whom they draw this key aspect of their identity. Thus, a right relationship with the sovereign, universal God is a central component of Israelite identity. And the veracity and vitality of this relationship is manifest in acts of *ḥesed*.

THE RUTH NARRATIVE'S RELEVANCE IN THE PERSIAN PERIOD

We now move beyond our primary focus on the world of the text. Which world we will explore depends on one's understanding of the provenance of the RN. If one holds that it was written earlier than Ezra-Nehemiah (EN),[52] it would primarily be an exploration of the world in front of the text—how a reader or hearer in the early Restoration period would understand the text within their own historical context.[53] If one holds that it was written around the time of EN, it would primarily be an exploration of the world behind the text—the social, political and ideological factors that influenced the writing of the RN and to which the

---

[52] Proponents of an earlier date include Block, *Judges, Ruth*; Campbell, *Ruth*; Hubbard, *Ruth*; Moshe Weinfeld, "Ruth, Book of," in *Encyclopaedia Judaica* (Jerusalem: Keter Publishing House, 1996).

[53] For those who hold that the RN was written prior to EN, the analogies between the RN and EN enhance the relevance of Ruth in the early Restoration period, a time in which Israel was a colony of the Persian Empire. Both the RN and EN are narratives of 'return': Ruth and Naomi return from Moab, a group of Yehudites return from Babylon. It is an adjustment period for characters in both narratives. Naomi's situation, as an Israelite repatriate, parallels that of the "returnees" who were exiled to Babylon but now return to their ancestral lands. Ruth's experience as a newcomer to the land of Israel most closely parallels the experience of those Yehudites born in Babylon and returning to a foreign "home" for the first time.

RN is partly a response.⁵⁴ I will take the latter position in the following discussion.

In EN the repatriates found themselves in a situation of extreme threat to Israelite identity and existence. This threat derived not only from Persian imperialism, but also from "the people of the land" (Ezra 4:4; עם הארץ). Although the term is used neutrally or positively elsewhere in the Old Testament,⁵⁵ in EN it has taken on a pejorative tinge,⁵⁶ referring to the resident population in Yehud. They are in contradistinction to EN's construction of "true Israel"—those who have returned from exile.⁵⁷ Within this context the RN can be read from a postcolonial perspective to preserve some elements of Israelite identity and freedom, but at the same time to resist other elements of Israelite identity and imperial rule.

The RN provides a subtle protest against ethnocentrism as central to Israelite identity. Some propose that the prohibition of intermarriage in the Persian Period mainly served the interests of imperial social control.⁵⁸ According to these scholars, genealogical purity was a way of establishing land tenure for the returnees, thereby asserting control of land and property. If this was a factor, then the RN would undermine this aspect of Persian policy. I maintain elsewhere, however, that the need to protect Israelite identity was probably the driving influence.⁵⁹ Whichever factor(s) were involved, the RN protests against the ideology of Israelite ethnic purity. Although, in the RN, marriage to a non-YHWH-fearing foreigner can lead to punishment (as illustrated in

---

⁵⁴ Recent proponents of a late date for the book of Ruth include Tamara Cohn Eskenazi and Tikva Simone Frymer-Kensky, *Ruth*, JPS Bible Commentary (Philadephia: Jewish Publication Society, 2011), xvi–xix; LaCocque, *Ruth*; Victor H. Matthews, *Judges/Ruth*, NCBC (Cambridge: Cambridge University Press, 2004); Ziony Zevit, "Dating Ruth: Legal, Linguistic and Historical Observations," *ZAW* 117 (2005).

⁵⁵ On עם הארץ in the HB, see, *inter alios*, Sara Japhet, "People and Land in the Restoration Period," in *From the Rivers of Babylon to the Highlands of Judah: Collected Studies on the Restoration Period* (Winona Lake: Eisenbrauns, 2006), 96–116; Ernest W. Nicholson, "The Meaning of the Expression עם הארץ in the Old Testament," *JSS* 10 (1965): 59–66.

⁵⁶ For a suggested diachronic development of the phrase, see E. Lipiński, *TDOT* 11:175.

⁵⁷ According to EN there is only one Israelite community in Yehud, the returned exiles (Ezra 2:1; Neh 7:6; cf. 4:1; 6:19, 20; 8:35; 9:4; 10:6, 7, 8, 16).

⁵⁸ Seminally, Kenneth G. Hoglund, *Achaemenid Imperial Administration in Syria-Palestine and the Missions of Ezra and Nehemiah* (Atlanta: Scholars Press, 1992).

⁵⁹ See Lau, *Identity and Ethics*, 159–65.

Mahlon and Chilion), marriage to a YHWH-fearing foreigner *is* permitted.⁶⁰ The crucial aspect of Israelite identity is a right (and exclusive) relationship with YHWH expressed in acts of *ḥesed*, not one's ethnicity. In fact, although muted, a hint of an inclusive outlook may be detected in EN's mention of foreigners participating in the Passover (Ezra 6:19–21) and in the community pledge to follow the Torah (Neh 10:29[28]).⁶¹ The RN would support this ethnic inclusiveness.

Closely allied to this inclusiveness is the RN's promotion of an expansive application of the Torah as integral to Israelite identity. In EN the Torah was characteristically used as an instrument of prohibition and restriction, with those infringing its laws facing state-sanctioned punishment (e.g., Ezra 7:26). The law's application in regards to intermarriage reinforces this perception (Ezra 9–10; Neh 13:23–31).⁶² The RN resists such a strict, ethnocentric application of the law; it presents, instead, a generous application of the law according to the principle of *ḥesed* and focuses on the moral logic underlying the law. This would reinforce an uncharacteristic application of the law found in Neh 5. Here Nehemiah's call for an immediate cancellation of debts and return of property does not follow the strict regulations of the שמטה (Deut 15:1–6; cf. Exod 23:10–11) or the Jubilee (Lev 25:8–55).⁶³ Instead, Nehemiah

---

⁶⁰ Deuteronomy prohibits marriage to foreign women because of the risk of apostasy (Deut 7:3–4). Reading the RN in dialogue with this text leads to the conclusion that Mahlon and Chilion's marriage to foreign women led them to suffer YHWH's punishment. Judgment did not befall Boaz because Ruth had already turned to YHWH (Ruth 1:16–17; cf. 2:12).

⁶¹ See Peter H. W. Lau, "Gentile Incorporation into Israel in Ezra–Nehemiah?" *Bib* 90 (2009): 356–73.

⁶² The differences between the two accounts are also noted, e.g., by Daniel L. Smith-Christopher, "The Mixed Marriage Crisis in Ezra 9–10 and Nehemiah 13: A Study of the Sociology of the Post-Exilic Judean Community," in *Second Temple Studies*, ed. Tamara C. Eshkenazi and Kent Richards, JSOTSup 175 (Atlanta: Scholars Press, 1994), 243–65. Both accounts, however, specifically name Moabites as among Israel's archetypal enemies (Ezra 9:1; Neh 13:1; cf. 13:23), drawing on Deut 7 and 23:3–6. On the use of Deuteronomic laws in Ezra 9–10 and Neh 13:23–31, see, inter alios, Michael Fishbane, *Biblical Interpretation in Ancient Israel* (Oxford: Clarendon, 1975), 115–28; Csilla Saysell, "Deuteronomy in the Intermarriage Crises in Ezra-Nehemiah," in *Interpreting Deuteronomy: Issues and Approaches*, ed. David G. Firth and Philip S. Johnston (Nottingham: IVP, 2012), 197–208.

⁶³ Some suggest that the legislation in Lev 25 had not yet been formulated. Rather, the laws in Lev 25 were drafted in response to situations like that found

appeals to the Jewish nobles and officials' sense of morality—"the thing you are doing is 'not good'" (לא טוב; 5:9). Nehemiah's main concern is the underlying morality of the creditors' behavior rather than strict legal observance. Hence, righteous behavior in accordance with the law's perceived intentions, rather than its specific stipulations, is presented as a key manifestation of Israelite identity.

The RN's presentation of YHWH's sovereignty has a number of effects on Israelite identity in the Restoration period. First, it reinforces dependence upon YHWH as an appropriate response for an Israelite. In the face of an apparently unstoppable and omnipresent Persian Empire,[64] within which Yehud was but one province, the RN affirms that God is in fact sovereign and omnipresent to act. That YHWH can even act in the everyday affairs of the people—apart from overt displays of power—would be germane to an Israelite living at a time when the Persian military advance on Egypt was probably an important imperial influence (539–522 BCE).[65] With the RN's affirmation of YHWH's background providence, Israelites can confidently place their trust in YHWH. They do not need to live a life of uncertainty, of divided allegiance.

Second, YHWH's sovereignty in the RN decenters the temple as fundamental to Israelite identity in the Restoration period. The temple was important in the Restoration period, as underlined in EN by its continuity with the Solomonic temple, priests, and temple personnel,[66] and its pivotal position to the overall movement of EN.[67] But the RN demonstrates that it is possible for YHWH-fearers to express their faith without the state-sponsored temple and cult.[68] YHWH is still present in the lives of Israelites in the absence of a physical sanctuary. Indeed, as John Berquist points out, the efficacy of the many prayers in the RN, independent of the temple and intermediaries such as priests, can be

---

in Neh 5; so, e.g., John W. Rogerson, *A Theology of the Old Testament: Cultural Memory, Communication, and Being Human* (Minneapolis: Fortress, 2010), 126–131.

[64] Jon L. Berquist, "Resistance and Accommodation in the Persian Empire," in *In the Shadow of Empire: Reclaiming the Bible as a History of Faithful Resistance*, ed. Richard A. Horsley (Louisville: Westminster John Knox, 2008), 44.

[65] Cf. Berquist, "Resistance," 47.

[66] E.g., Ezra 2:36–58; 6:18; Neh 12:24, 45–46. Cf. H. G. M. Williamson, *Ezra, Nehemiah* (Waco, TX: Word, 1985), 82–84.

[67] Tamara C. Eskenazi, *In an Age of Prose: A Literary Approach to Ezra-Nehemiah* (Atlanta: Scholars Press, 1988), 38–39.

[68] Persian patronage for temple and cult can be found in Ezra 3:7; 6:9; 7:15–17, 22; Neh 2:8.

viewed as a form of resistance.[69] By demonstrating alternative religious practices, the RN undermines the hegemony of the Persian Empire.

Finally, the presentation of YHWH's sovereignty in RN raises the hope for native imperial rule as a component of Israelite identity. The RN reminds Israelites living in the Restoration period that they are heirs of the Davidic promise, and thus ignites aspirations for a re-establishment of the Davidic monarchy.[70] It is a reminder that Israel's ideal ruler is a YHWH-installed king "from amongst their brothers" (cf. Deut 17:14–20). If EN represents the voice of the ruling urban elite installed by Persia, as embodied in Ezra, Nehemiah, the priests, and governors, then the sentiments at the end of the prayer in Neh 9 can be read as an outcome of cultural mimicry.[71] Although externally affirming the ruling structure, the elite concurrently place a suppressed challenge in the mouths of the Levites, who lament the nation's suffering under the hand of a foreign king (Neh 9:36–37), and a longing for God to return them to a time of rule under their "own king" (Neh 9:35).[72] A negative portrayal of Persian rule can be found in the other two major prayers in Ezra-Nehemiah (Ezra 6; Neh 1), not just in the prayer in Nehemiah 9.[73] The prayers thus subvert the grip of imperial power, and look forward to a time of independent Davidic rule.

Conclusion

I have argued that, from a postcolonial perspective, examining the world of the text is a fruitful line of enquiry. This enquiry revealed that Israelite ethnic identity is subsumed by religious identity—an identity based on a right relationship with YHWH, the sovereign provider and protector of

---

[69] Cf. Berquist, "Resistance," 55. That is not to say that the priests function purely as agents of the Persian Empire.
[70] For a presentation of the case that the RN anticipates David and his house, see Greg Goswell, "The Book of Ruth and the House of David," *EvQ* 86 (2014): 116–29.
[71] For a description of "mimicry" in postcolonial studies, see Homi K. Bhabha, *The Location of Culture* (London: Routledge, 1994), 85–92.
[72] Cf. Daniel L. Smith-Christopher, *A Biblical Theology of Exile* (Minneapolis: Fortress, 2002), 44–45. David is not named specifically, as would be expected for a document written under the watch of another power. The effect of the allusion is that the Davidic hope is muted. For the contrary view, see Greg Goswell, "The Absence of a Davidic Hope in Ezra-Nehemiah," *TJ* 33 (2012): 19–31.
[73] Greg Goswell, "The Attitude to the Persians in Ezra-Nehemiah," *TJ* 32 (2011): 191–203 (198–201).

all people. The RN also emphasizes the importance of living out this relationship with YHWH, the universally sovereign God, as expressed in acts of *ḥesed*. These themes in the RN resist ideologies found in the world of the text itself. It was not necessary to identify a particular imperial power and then propose how the text responded to its domination. It was also not necessary to start with a foreign power to consider how it might have controlled the production of the text. That is not to say that a biblical text may not be a response to or is influenced by colonial rule. As shown above, the RN can be understood to contain elements of opposition against Persian domination.

But I maintain that any postcolonial reading must keep the concerns of the text central in order to maintain its hermeneutical integrity. Superimposing a postcolonial ideology (or any ideology) upon the biblical text can be a self-deconstructing move. By imposing a dominating reading strategy onto the text, the strategy becomes its own oppression; the voice of the text is suppressed by the grip of postcolonial ideology. As a burgeoning area in biblical studies, the trickle of postcolonial studies sensitive to the world of the text needs to become a more robust stream for postcolonial approaches to survive and leave a lasting mark.

THE KEY TO SUCCESSFUL MIGRATION? REREADING RUTH'S CONFESSION (1:16–17) THROUGH THE LENS OF BHABHA'S MIMICRY·

Sin-lung Tong

The book of Ruth is a survival story of three widows: Naomi, Ruth, and Orpah. It soon became the story of two widows, Naomi and Ruth, returning to Naomi's hometown. In Ruth's case, it was an opportunity to cling to Naomi in order to survive the loss of her loved ones and in order to secure their future. We imagine that Naomi and Ruth still had to struggle for their future, even though they were going back to Naomi's place of origin. Ruth not only had to worry about her basic needs, but she also had to adapt to a foreign culture, its people and its God. One may wonder how Ruth the Moabite was going to survive all these by just clinging to her mother-in-law. It is tempting to jump to the conclusion that God's providence saved the widows, directly by making Ruth conceive (Ruth 4:13) and indirectly through the human agent of God, namely, Boaz.[1] However, God did not call upon Ruth to confess and be converted. Neither did God command Boaz to act beyond the requirement of the Sinai Law and marry Ruth. There is actually more to say about the interactions between these characters.

Perhaps Boaz's kindness (חסד) is the key to Ruth's successful migration. Ruth's confession (Ruth 1:16–17) and her deeds of loyalty to Naomi play a significant role in their survival. One may again wonder what other perspectives we should apply to look into the story afresh.

In this chapter, I argue that Ruth's confession can be, in Homi Bhabha's terms, a mimicry, which, on the one hand, allows Ruth to win the trust of Boaz and, on the other hand, exposes the domination-subordination relationship between the hegemon and the immigrant.

· This chapter is a revision of a paper presented at the Society of Asian Biblical Studies meeting 2012 in Kota Kinabalu, Malaysia, and published in *CMS Journal* 13 (2013): 57–73. It has been revised and printed here with permission.
[1] Edward F. Campbell Jr., *Ruth,* AB (New York: Doubleday, 1975), 28–29.

Ruth's submission is part and parcel to her successful migration. Moreover, her confession and her deeds of loyalty also allow her to reclaim her subjectivity and pose challenges to the hegemon. I will also compare the case of Ruth with the current situation in Hong Kong to see if rereading Ruth's story may shed light on the problem we are facing.

RUTH'S COMMITMENT TO A FOREIGN PEOPLE AND GOD (RUTH 1:16–17)

Before Ruth swears her allegiance to the new people and new faith in Ruth 1:16–17, her mother-in-law had been trying to persuade Orpah and her to "return" (Ruth 1:8–9, 11–13, 15). Of all the fifteen occurrences of שׁוּב in the book of Ruth, twelve of them occur in chapter one, setting the stage for a survival story of three widows. Indeed, the theme of "return" is prominent. But to where could the three widows (re)turn?

Ruth's confession (Ruth 1:16–17) has been interpreted as her conversion from her past life and religion to a person who commits to the people and God of Israel. The Midrash Rabbah to the book of Ruth portrays Ruth as a fully resolved convert, who is even eager to embrace the "misfortunes" of her mother-in-law. By announcing her confession, Ruth is willing to turn away from her Gentile customs and embrace Israelite practices. Ruth Rabbah suggests that Ruth is willing to refrain from visiting "gentile theatres and circuses" as Naomi has requested. Thus, she says, "where you go, I will go." She is also determined to dwell only in houses that have their *mezuzot* or doorposts marked by the Lord's Shema (Deut 6:9). Thus, she says, "Where you lodge, I will lodge." Furthermore, Ruth's commitment undoubtedly includes her faithfulness to the torah and other commandments of the Bible.[2] Although many scholars reject Ruth's confession as a form of conversion or "judaization,"[3] Ruth's commitment expressed in her speech is evident and undeniable.

Ruth's confession also shares the covenantal language found in treaties between kings in ancient west Asia. I will not repeat the detailed comparison made by Mark S. Smith, but it is enough to state that both the international treaties and Ruth's speech have similar covenantal expressions. For example, Jehoshaphat's "my people are your people, my horses are your horses" (1 Kgs 22:4; 2 Kgs 3:7) resembles Ruth's "your people shall be my people, and your God my God" (1:16). Despite

---

[2] "Ruth, II.22" in *The Midrash Rabbah*, vol. 4, New Compact Edition (London: Soncino Press, 1977).
[3] Mark S. Smith, "'Your People Shall Be My People': Family and Covenant in Ruth 1:16–17," *CBQ* 69 (2007): 243–44.

the similarity of the language, Smith contends that there are fundamental differences between the covenants made internationally and those within a family. He also argues that Ruth's speech and even the whole book of Ruth do not emphasize the notion of her conversion. Instead, Ruth commits to her relationship with Naomi and her people within the context of a family.[4] We see again that Ruth's commitment is beyond question.

Ruth's commitment is further emphasized when she seals her confession with an oath formula in verse 17. There are twelve occurrences of such an oath formula with slight variations in the Hebrew Bible. Ten of them have the formula כה יעשה אלהים ... וכה יסיף. The remaining two, including the one in Ruth's confession, replace אלהים with the Tetragrammaton. Yael Ziegler asserts that this replacement in Ruth's confession is "a result of her understanding of what the personal deity of the people of Israel requires of her."[5] Although his take on the change of God's name is stretching it too much, I am inclined to agree with Ziegler that the use of the Tetragrammaton is deliberate and more persuasive to Naomi.[6]

Apparently, Ruth is committed to her mother-in-law as if she had already given some thought to it. One may think that Ruth has no other option, because her life depends on it. But the fact that Orpah chose to return to her mother's house indicates that there was still a chance of survival in the land of Moab. Nevertheless, the text does not mention explicitly why Ruth made such a commitment to a new people and a new God. One can continue to fill in the blanks, but all proposals will be speculations at best.[7] However, this gap in the narrative allows us to explore the possible meanings of Ruth's confession through a different mindset. Now I turn to the theory of postcolonialism and especially Homi Bhabha's theory of mimicry before coming back to Ruth's confession.

Postcolonialism and Bhabha's Mimicry

Postcolonialism aims to study "the relationship between center and margin, metropolis and periphery, on a global political scale—the

---

[4] Ibid, 256–57.
[5] Yael Ziegler, "'So Shall God Do...': Variations of an Oath Formula and Its Literary Meaning," *JBL* 126 (2007): 80.
[6] Ibid, 80.
[7] Katharine D. Sakenfeld, *Ruth: Interpretation: A Bible Commentary for Teaching and Preaching* (Louisville: Westminster John Knox, 1999), 33–34.

imperial and the colonial."[8] It covers a wide disciplinary range that can be defined in historic-political,[9] temporal,[10] psychosociological,[11] and linguistic terms and even in terms of its consequences.[12] Ulrike Sals points out two characteristics of postcolonial study. Firstly, it exposes the fallacy of stereotype(s) that defines cultural purity. Secondly, it seeks to reveal "the tension between metropolitan centers and the (ex/neo)colonial periphery."[13] When postcolonial theories are applied to biblical studies, Sals simply identifies west Asian superpowers such as Egypt, Assyria, Babylonia, or Persia as the metropolitan centers and Israel as the periphery.[14] While Sals does mention that "there are many marginalized persons and groups" within Israel,[15] John J. Collins reminds us that Israel was once a conqueror to the indigenous Canaanites. A "Canaanite perspective" is thus introduced in order to "appreciate 'the face of the other,' in the phrase of Emmanuel Lévinas, or to allow the subaltern to speak."[16] In short, postcolonialism generally assumes a tension between the colonizers who are characterized as the center with power and authority and the colonized as the peripheries being suppressed and even oppressed.

One must not simplify the relationship between the colonizer and the colonized. The colonizer seeks to portray the colonized as people with disabilities of some sort and justifies its conquest and governance as if they are doing something beneficial to the colonized.[17] At the same time, there is an anxiety in every colonizer, because its self-identity is being threatened by the same colonized people. While the colonizer celebrates its "virtue" of inclusiveness or "multiculturalism," it betrays its anxiety in the process of suppressing the voices of the colonized. David Huddart aptly captures what Homi Bhabha suggests is the interrelatedness between the colonizer and the colonized: "If you stare at

---

[8] Fernando F. Segovia, "Postcolonial and Diasporic Criticism in Biblical Studies: Focus, Parameters, Relevance," *Studies in World Christianity* 5 (1999): 180.
[9] Ibid, 180–81.
[10] Ibid, 181.
[11] Ibid.
[12] Ulrike Sals, "The Hybrid Story of Balaam (Numbers 22–24): Theology for the Diaspora in the Torah," *Biblical Interpretation* 16 (2008): 318.
[13] Ibid.
[14] Ibid, 318–19.
[15] Ibid, 319.
[16] John J. Collins, *The Bible After Babel: Historical Criticism in a Postmodern Age* (Grand Rapids: Eerdmans, 2005), 65–66.
[17] Homi K. Bhabha, *The Location of Culture*, 2nd edition (London: Routledge, 2004), 100–101.

people it might seem that you have fixed them in place, but of course they will always look back and threaten your sense of self: in other words, self and other are locked together."[18]

This gazing-back of the colonized shakes the foundation of the colonial discourse that tries to fix the stereotyped object(s) in a frozen misrepresentation. Thus, one must resist the gaze of the colonizer by gazing back, so that those being gazed upon may reclaim their subjectivity. Any discourse or discursive act will only become too powerful if we allow them to achieve their effects. This is where Bhabha's mimicry comes into play to resist the colonial discourse.

Bhabha's mimicry is a form of gazing back and a way to reclaim subjectivity. Mimicry may look like an imitation on the surface, risking the colonized being assimilated into the dominant or colonial culture. It is in fact "a repetition with difference" and "a form of mockery."[19] While colonial discourse pretends to educate and improve the "inferior" conditions of the colonized, mimicry undermines this frozen stereotype by exposing its slippage and ambivalence. Moreover, mimicry turns the colonized or the "inferior" into an agency, threatening the so-called "norm."[20] The colonized may not be consciously acting like an agency or "adopting mimicry as a deliberate *strategy*."[21] Instead, the colonial discourse generates its own mimicry, shaking its own foundation of the colonizer's superiority. As a matter of fact, the colonizer needs to justify its ruling over the colonized by "educating" them. While the colonized is being "educated," the colonized becomes "almost the same, but not quite" as its superior. Consequently, the superior becomes anxious when it sees its doppelgangers. Mimicry is indeed a haunting ghost that constantly makes the colonizer anxious. As Bhabha puts it succinctly, "the ambivalence of colonial authority repeatedly turns from *mimicry*—a difference that is almost nothing but not quite—to *menace*—a difference that is almost total but not quite."[22]

The fact that this change from mimicry to menace is a repeating process reminds us of the shaky foundation of colonial rule. The "education" that the colonized obtain constantly undermines the superiority of the colonizer. As a result, the colonizer always has to invent new identities in order to justify their domination.

---

[18] David Huddart, *Homi K. Bhabha* (London: Routledge, 2006), 29.
[19] Ibid, 39.
[20] Bhabha, *Location of Culture*, 122–23.
[21] Huddart, *Homi K. Bhabha*, 41.
[22] Bhabha, *Location of Culture*, 131.

Rereading Ruth's Confession

Through the lens of postcolonial theory and Bhabha's mimicry, we reread Ruth's confession afresh. From Ruth 1:22 onwards we observe that Ruth is labeled as "the Moabite." This label, whether given by the narrator or the people of Israel, functions like a stereotyping device that discriminates the center and the periphery, the superior and the inferior. The Moabite label reminds the readers of the particular stipulation that no Moabite, even to the tenth generation, shall be admitted to the assembly of the Lord (Deut 23:3). The Israelites will never forget how they were once seduced sexually and that they were invited to worship the Moabite gods at Shittim (Num 25:1–3). We must not fail to mention that Balak, the Moabite king hired Balaam to curse the people of Israel (Num 22–24). Recalling these Israelite encounters with the Moabites is sufficient for readers to imagine how the Moabite label sounds to an Israelite community. Ruth the Moabite is obviously the periphery, if not the outcast. While one may think that Ruth's confession would help her blend in more easily, the recurring Moabite label proves otherwise. This label, in Bhabha's terms, is a fixed stereotype that keeps Ruth in a frozen misrepresentation.

By contrast, Boaz the prominent rich man in the community seems a bit unconventional at first sight. He does not use the Moabite label, but calls Ruth, "my daughter," in the same way that Naomi does (Ruth 2:7). Boaz's kind words and even protection offered to Ruth (Ruth 2:8–9, 14–16) appear to be an unconditional "favor" (חן) as Ruth initially sees it (Ruth 2:10, 13). Yet, Boaz recounts Ruth's loyal deeds to her mother-in-law in his comment (Ruth 2:11–12). The notion of loyalty is made explicit later when Boaz talks to Ruth a second time at the threshing floor and praises her for her better "loyalty" (חסד) than the first (Ruth 3:10).[23] "Loyalty" is a totally different concept than "favor." Katharine Sakenfeld rightly points out that "loyalty" refers to an action essential to the basic well-being of the recipients, provided by a person with appropriate position, and within the context of an existing and positive relationship.[24] Thus, "loyalty" assumes a patron-recipient relationship with different socioeconomic positions. Boaz and Naomi are the patrons and the center in the community. Boaz has the economic resources and social position, whereas Naomi has at least the social connection. In contrast, Ruth has nothing to offer but her availability. Yet she has been loyal to her

---

[23] Sakenfeld, *Ruth*, 61.
[24] Ibid, 24.

mother-in-law and even shows greater loyalty to Boaz. What can we make of such loyalty?

This is where Bhabha's mimicry can help us make sense of Ruth's confession and her commitment to a relationship that discriminates between the center and the periphery, the patron and the recipient. Assuming that Ruth's confession is a pledge to commit herself to a relationship with Naomi, this pledge might as well be a vow to submit to a domination-subordination relationship. This submission becomes evident when we compare Ruth's speeches in 1:16, 17, and 3:5. The syntax in these sentences is strikingly similar as shown below:

1:16ba	אל־אשר תלכי אלך
1:16bb	באשר תליני אלין
1:17a	באשר תמותי אמות
3:5	כל אשר־תאמרי אעשה

Each of the four sentences consists of a relative particle with an imperfect verb form in second person feminine singular, followed by another imperfect verb form in first person singular. While the first three sentences express Ruth's commitment to an intimate relationship, the fourth is a submissive response from Ruth, who acts like a subordinate toward a superior. If the first part of the fourth sentence is a command by Naomi, the similar syntax of the first three sentences may also suggest imperative actions that Ruth has to follow. Thus, one can take Ruth's confession (Ruth 1:16–17) as a vow of submission. Yet this same vow can also be a mimicry that exposes the slippery foundation of the superior, and turns the subordinate into an agency. By her vow of submission, Ruth bows to the superiority of the people and the God of Israel. At the same time, her vow becomes a challenge to the center or the patron of the community, asking whether he or she could live up to the expectation of being a superior.

Mark Smith points out that one of the differences between Ruth's confession and an international treaty is the word order. When Jehoshaphat says "my people are your people, my horses are your horses" (1 Kgs 22:4), he is determined to fight and is prepared to share his military resources with the king of Israel. In contrast, Ruth's confession has a different word order, putting the people and the God of Israel first. The reversed word order suggests, in Smith's opinion, "what is Naomi's will be Ruth's."[25] Thus, the vow of submission is a mimicry

---

[25] Smith, "Your People Shall Be My People," 256–57.

that poses the challenge to the people and the God of Israel: how will the people and the God of Israel take care of a marginalized immigrant? In short, the superior is reminded through this mimicry that he or she is held accountable for the well-being of its subordinate.

Bhabha also reminds us that the change from "mimicry" to "menace" is a repeating process. His theory offers us an intriguing perspective to read the story of Ruth afresh. Ruth's confession sets off the cycle that haunts the superior in the community. When everyone in the community gazes at Ruth by reminding her of her Moabite origin, the fact that she has lived up to her confession "gazes" back at the community. Her loyalty to Naomi proves her capable of being more than a Moabite label that defines and confines her. Ruth's action undermines the superiority of the people of Israel. Suddenly, this Moabite and the Israelites are not so different after all.

The story reminds us that the Israelites have the Sinai law that takes care of the alien, the poor, the orphan, and the widow (Lev 19:9–10; Deut 24:19–22). This is probably why Ruth the Moabite is allowed to glean in the field (Ruth 2:3, 7). Boaz the prominent rich man even goes beyond the prescribed law and offers Ruth extra protection from any possible "unsolicited advances by men in the area" (Ruth 2:8–9, 14–16).[26] Once again, the superiority is reestablished. Yet, Boaz the prominent rich man is caught off guard again by Ruth's subsequent submission to Naomi's inconceivable suggestion of seducing Boaz at the threshing floor (Ruth 3:1–5). This time, Ruth's submissive action as a mimicry is coupled with her proposal speech in Ruth 3:9. Her "menace" challenges Boaz to take up his responsibility of a next-of-kin to marry her. From then onwards, Ruth's fate sadly comes out of her grasp, as her future security is determined by a group of men at the city gate. We no longer hear from Ruth but witness her son being taken away from her bosom (Ruth 4:16). Even her right to name her son is removed from her (Ruth 4:17). Ruth disappears from the stage until her name resurfaces in Jesus's genealogy (Matt 1:5).

Although the ending of the story is disappointing, we must not undermine the contribution of Bhabha's mimicry to our rereading of Ruth's confession. The mimicry in her confession, on one hand, exposes the domination-subordination relationship between the Israelite community and the Moabite immigrant and, on the other hand, becomes a menace that shakes the foundation of the stereotype. The hegemon will certainly try different ways to stabilize the domination-subordination relationship. However, the anxiety that the repeating mimicry/menace

---

[26] Sakenfeld, *Ruth*, 43.

cycle generated can provide the necessary space for the marginalized, the alien or immigrant to resist and perhaps survive.

MIMICRY OF HONG KONG PEOPLE

This rereading of Ruth's confession seems irrelevant to Hong Kong's current situation. It has been sixteen years since Hong Kong was returned to the People's Republic of China by Great Britain. While Ruth apparently had the choice to cling to Naomi, many of the Hong Kong citizens did not get to choose but only to accept the return of Hong Kong to the sovereignty of China.[27] However, Ruth's social status as a Moabite in an Israelite community is not unlike that of the status of Hong Kong in her relationship with China. Although the Joint Declaration made by China and Britain in 1984 states that the city will be run by the people of Hong Kong for fifty years under the principle of "One Country, Two Systems," the Hong Kong Government is gradually giving up the distinction between "Two Systems" and is eager to assimilate itself with the Central Government of China into "One Country."[28]

The recent election of the new chief executive of Hong Kong reveals how proestablishment camps in the political arena as well as in the media are willing to do what it takes to please the Central Government of China. For example, an opinion piece by commentator Johnny Lau was unfairly edited and distorted by the Sing Pao Daily News, favoring Mr. Leung Chun-ying, one of the Hong Kong chief executive candidates.[29] During the election period, one of the local newspapers had also received numerous calls from the Chinese Liaison Office in Hong Kong, the primary agent for the Central Government of China in the territory, and was castigated for their in-depth report on Mr. Leung.[30]

---

[27] British Consulate-General Hong Kong, "British Nationality (Hong Kong) Act 1997," UK in Hong Kong, http://ukinhongkong.fco.gov.uk/en/help-for-british-nationals/living-in-hong-kong/ethnic-minorities/.

[28] Kenneth Ka-lok Chan, "Taking Stock of One Country, Two Systems," in *"One Country, Two Systems" in Crisis: Hong Kong's Transformation Since the Handover*, ed. Yiu-chung Wong (Lanham: Lexington Books, 2004), 44–49.

[29] Rosa Trieu, "Hongkongers' Press Freedom Threatened by China's Creeping Influence," *Forbes*, June 25, 2012, http://www.forbes.com/sites/rosatrieu/2012/06/25/hongkongers-press-freedom-threatened-by-chinas-creeping-influence/2/.

[30] IFJ Asia-Pacific, "Mainland Interference in Political Reporting Alleged in Hong Kong," *International Federation of Journalists*, March 22, 2012, http://asiapacific.ifj.org/en/articles/mainland-interference-in-political-reporting-alleged-in-hong-kong.

The political stance of the proestablishment camps is no mimicry whatsoever but simply a self-castration and surrender. In contrast, those whose political views are not in harmony with those of the Central Government of China are marginalized.[31]

The discrimination between the center and the periphery, the hegemon and the subordinate appears to be present in the relation between the Central Government of China and Hong Kong, as in the story of Ruth. The nature of the relationship between the Central Government of China and Hong Kong people is similar to the one between the Israelite community and Ruth. In short, Hong Kong people have never been freed from being colonized, and the rereading of Ruth can lend itself to our understanding of Hong Kong's current situation.

Archie Lee once wrote, "Postcolonialism does not necessarily oppose and radically reject a former colonial legacy."[32] A recent survey conducted by the Hong Kong Institute of Asia-Pacific Studies of the Chinese University of Hong Kong supports Lee's assertion: of the 878 persons surveyed, 66 percent considered that the British Colonial Government did a better job than the Hong Kong Government after 1997.[33] Leo Goodstadt, the head of Central Policy Unit to the British Colonial Government up to 1 July, 1997, pointedly comments that the people born in 1980's or after received the best education in Hong Kong's history but also have the worst employment conditions and prospects.[34] The people in Hong Kong are discontented with the government for the latter is considered to be incompetent in tackling the housing, political, economic, and education problems. It is no wonder that the Hong Kong people do not radically reject the British Colonial

---

[31] Since the Alliance for Universal Suffrage (AUS) negotiated with authorities in Hong Kong and Beijing for a compromised political reform package, Beijing marginalized the more radical Civil Party and League of Social Democrats by branding the prodemocracy camps involved in AUS as "moderate democrats." See Kin Man Chan, "Cleavages and Challenges in Hong Kong's Pro-Democracy Camp," *Hong Kong Journal* 22 (July 2011): 2–3, http://www.hkjournal.org/PDF/2011_fall/3.pdf.

[32] Chichang Li, "Returning to China : Biblical Interpretation in Postcolonial Hong Kong," *Biblical Interpretation* 7 (Apr 1999): 165.

[33] Hong Kong Institute of Asia-Pacific Studies, "Survey on How Hong Kong People Feel about the Status Quo after Handover to China since 1997 (2011)," http://www.cuhk.edu.hk/hkiaps/tellab/pdf/telepress/11/Press_Release_20110628.pdf.

[34] Hong Kong Connection, "14 Years On—The Hong Kong SAR," Radio Television Hong Kong, http://programme.rthk.org.hk/rthk/tv/programme.php?name=tv/hkce&d=2011-10-06&p=1981&e=154313&m=episode.

Government. They even romanticize about the British Colonial Government.

The new hegemon to Hong Kong is no different to any others. In fact, all hegemons will try whatever means necessary to keep their subordinates under control. Despite the political setbacks in Hong Kong, the Central Government offers the people of Hong Kong a "Closer Economic Partnership Arrangement" ("CEPA") so that Hong Kong remains competitive in terms of trading and investment. Ironically, many people in Hong Kong do not benefit from these economic sweeteners. Indeed, about 58 percent of the people interviewed in the Hong Kong Institute of Asia-Pacific Studies survey have indicated that the Hong Kong economy has worsened after the return to China.[35] The Central Government of China offers support to the Hong Kong Government and demands that it keep its citizens in harmony and subordination.[36]

The Hong Kong Government could actually be a mimicry by itself, but it dares not to be "almost the same, but not quite." The Hong Kong Government simply receives orders from the Central Government of China, but fails to step forward for its people to act as an active agent in voicing out their concerns namely housing, political, economic, education and more. For example, Hong Kong government has been reluctant to speak for the prodemocracy camps regarding the issue of universal suffrage. Instead, the Hong Kong government acted solely as a mouthpiece of Beijing.[37] Consequently, some of the Hong Kong people choose a more radical way to protest. For instance, lawmaker Wong Yuk-man from the People Power has threatened to oppose the government's

---

[35] Hong Kong Institute of Asia-Pacific Studies, "Survey on How Hong Kong People Feel about the Status Quo after Handover to China Since 1997 (2011)," http://www.cuhk.edu.hk/hkiaps/tellab/pdf/telepress/11/Press_Release_20110628.pdf.

[36] Chinese President Hu Jintao expressed concerns of "deep disagreements" in Hong Kong society as he swore in the new Hong Kong Chief Executive Mr. Leung. See Tan Ee Lyn and James Pomfret, "Crowds Protest in Hong Kong as Hu Anoints Leader," *Reuters*, July 2, 2012, http://in.reuters.com/article/2012/07/02/hongkong-china-idINDEE86102Y20120702.

[37] The compromise between Hong Kong's democrats and Central Government of China on the political reform in 2010 seems to bring greater democracy in the territory. It, however, falls short of the demand of universal suffrage in 2012 and scrapping of the functional constituencies. See The Economist Group, "Elections in Hong Kong: Functionally Democratic," *The Economist*, 24 June 2010, http://www.economist.com/node/16439175.

policies by filibustering and even more "bodily" means of protest.[38] Others become apathetic to political issues as long as their living standards are not adversely affected.

In contrast, Ruth exemplifies the use of the mimicry/menace cycle, although the story shows no sign of her using it consciously and strategically. Ruth still provides Hong Kong people an imagination for survival and adaptation. After all, it is a fact that Hong Kong is a part of China and does not seek independence. The Hong Kong Government and its citizens have the option to be active agents that are proud to be a part of China but willing to show that they are different from the Mainland in how they engage politically.

Conclusion

Through the lens of Bhabha's mimicry, we observe a totally different perspective of the story, particularly of Ruth's confession. This perspective, I must emphasize, is not the only way for us to read the story. Neither does it replace the traditional interpretation of the story, emphasizing the themes of divine providence through human agencies, deeds of loyalty and the like. The lens of Bhabha's mimicry, nevertheless, allows us to see how a typically marginalized outsider survives possible struggles and perhaps even challenges the dominant culture. In this chapter, Ruth's mimicry is taken as a source of imagination for Hong Kong people to rethink their relationship with China.

---

[38] Tony Cheung, "People Power Warns of Heavy Tactics to Get Its Point Across in Legco," *South China Morning Post*, October 9, 2012.

"Who Is More to You than Seven Sons": A Cross-Textual Reading between the Book of Ruth and *A Pair of Peacocks to the Southeast Fly*

Yan Lin

Ruth's kindness to her mother-in-law in the book of Ruth is highly praised in Judeo-Christian tradition, and their friendship is approved also.[1] Moreover, the book of Ruth is the only text that directly talks about the relationship between mother-in-law and daughter-in-law in the Hebrew Bible, so readers have a strong impression that a good relationship between mother-in-law and daughter-in-law is the norm, just like that of Naomi and Ruth.[2] But as a Chinese female reader who is deeply influenced by Confucianism, I have to be skeptical about such a wonderful relationship.

Contemporary Chinese women no longer need to observe "the three obediences and the four virtues;"[3] nonetheless, these are still practiced in China today. I think these "obediences and virtues" are still kept for the following reasons. Firstly, most Chinese parents traditionally buy houses for their sons when they get married. Thus, newly married wives live in these houses with their husbands and their parents-in-law. Secondly, sons are expected to support their parents in their old age, so most Chinese think that daughters-in-law should look after their husbands' parents, while sons-in-law do not need to. Chinese women often feel

---

[1] Julie L. C. Chu, "Returning Home: The Inspiration of the Role Dedifferentiation in the Book of Ruth for Taiwanese Women," *Semeia* 1997 (78): 47–53.

[2] Besides the relationship between Naomi and Ruth, Esau married foreigners who made life bitter for Rebekah (Gen 26:35), which indirectly reflects the relationship between mother-in-law and daughter-in-law. The story of Judah and Tamar (Gen 38) reflects the relationship between father-in-law and daughter-in-law.

[3] "The three obediences and the four virtues" is the ancient Chinese order of feudal society. "Three obediences" are that a female obeys her father before marriage, her husband when married, and her sons in widowhood. "Four virtues" include morality, proper speech, a modest manner, and diligent work.

pressure from their husbands' parents because of Chinese cultural tradition and women's perceived economic inferiority. Chinese women usually take care of domestic matters, so daughters-in-law's pressure mainly comes from their mothers-in-law.

There are many examples in Chinese literature that reflect the difficult relationship between mother-in-law and daughter-in-law.[4] One famous example is the long narrative poem, *A Pair of Peacocks to the Southeast Fly* (196–220 CE),[5] which has long been embodied in the text book of Chinese language and literature for senior middle school students. This is a preface to the poem:

> During the years of Jian'an (A.D. 196–220) at the close of the Han Dynasty, Liu Lanzhi, the wife of Jiao Zhongqing, a minor official in the prefecture of Lujiang, was dismissed by her mother-in-law. She vowed that she would never marry again. Coerced by her family to get remarried, she committed suicide by drowning herself in a pond. Upon hearing the news, Jiao Zhongqing also committed suicide by hanging himself on a tree in his courtyard. A contemporary poet felt deep sympathy for him and thus composed a poem.[6]

Considering Chinese women's experience, this chapter will reread the relationship between Naomi and Ruth from the perspective of *A Pair of Peacocks to the Southeast Fly*. The analysis will focus on Naomi's two speeches and two silences and examine Naomi's inner world in light of the Chinese poem.

Naomi's First Speech

When Naomi decided to return to Bethlehem, she said to her two daughters-in-law:

---

[4] Other examples include: *Field* (1937), *The Golden Chain* (1943), *Bitter Cold Nights* (1947), *Meng Xiangying's Emancipating* (1947), and *Double-Sided Tapes* (2010).

[5] There are three titles of this poem. The original is *An Old Poem Composed for the Wife of Jiao Zhongqing (With a Preface)—Jade Newly Chants*, and the earliest evidence of the use of this title is in *Yu Tai Xin Yong (Jade Newly Chants)*, edited by Chen Xuling (502–557 CE). The second title is *The Bride of Jiao Zhongqing—The Folk Poetry Collection*, which appeared in *Yu Fu Shi Ji (The Folk Poetry Collection)*, edited by Guo Maoqian (1031–1099 CE). The third title is *A Pair of Peacocks to the Southeast Fly*, translated by Wang Rongpei and appeared in *300 Early Chinese Poems (206 BCE–618 CE)* (Changsha: Hunan People's Publishing House, 2006), 102.

[6] Rongpei, *300 Early Chinese Poems*, 103.

> Turn back, my daughters, why will you go with me? Do I still have sons in my womb that they may become your husbands? Turn back, my daughters, go your way, for I am too old to have a husband. Even if I thought there was hope for me, even if I should have a husband tonight and bear sons, would you then wait until they were grown? Would you then refrain from marrying? No, my daughters, it has been far more bitter for me than for you, because the hand of the Lord has turned against me. (Ruth 1:11–13)

Naomi clearly knew her situation: she was old and well advanced in years, and she had no husband and no sons. In ancient Israel, marriage and sons provide security and a sense of self-worth.[7] But now that there were no men in her family, she thought, "the hand of the Lord has turned against me" (Ruth 1:13). With self-mockery, Naomi states that if only she could bear sons who would marry her daughters-in-law, which was actually the requirement of Levite marriage:

> When brothers reside together, and one of them dies and has no son, the wife of the deceased shall not be married outside the family to a stranger. Her husband's brother shall go in to her, taking her in marriage, and performing the duty of a husband's brother to her. (Deut 25:5)

As we read these moving words, we begin to understand Naomi's miserable life.

But when we analyze the reason that Liu Lanzhi was dismissed by Jiao Zhongqing's mother in the Chinese poem, we gain a different insight into Naomi's words. Zhongqing's mother complained to her son: "This wife of yours has been led astray; Whate'er she does, she does in her own way." Thus, she persuades her son: "It's best to send Lanzhi home right away; at our home she may no longer stay!" Taking the words of Zhongqing's mother literally, she had to do it for the simple reason that she hated Lanzhi's strong self-awareness and her refusal to being governed. But when we carefully read the verse "since our marriage, not three years yet are past," we can understand why Lanzhi was in an awkward situation in her husband's family: she still did not bear any children after years of marriage. Therefore, in my opinion, the

---

[7] Amy-Jill Levine, "Ruth," in *Women's Bible Commentary (Expanded Edition)*, ed. Carol A. Newsom and Sharon H. Ringe (Louisville: Westminster John Knox, 1998), 86.

underlying reason that Zhongqing's mother dismissed Lanzhi is Lanzhi's barrenness.

The Ancient Chinese book, *Da Dai Li Ji* (100–150 CE), records many reasons for divorcing one's wife. These reasons include disobeying a husband's parents, bearing no sons, pruriency, jealousy, foul disease, multiloquence, and theft.[8] The first, disobeying, is subjective, but bearing no sons is objective and cannot be concealed. Even if Lanzhi has countless advantages, we can be sure that she cannot please her mother-in-law because of her barrenness. There is further evidence, such as when Lanzhi farewelled her sister-in-law with these words: "Chu qi and Xia jiu, remember me while you sing and play." "Chu qi" is the seventh day of Chinese lunar July, and "Xia jiu" is the nineteenth day of every month, both of these are ancient Chinese festivals. The former was set for unmarried girls, who acted as a "go-between" on a moonlit night, whereby they hoped to obtain the recognition of future mother-in-laws;[9] the latter was for married women who enjoyed a happy get-together and worshipped the Songzi goddess to bear more sons. Lanzhi mentioned these two festivals with the hope that her mother-in-law would accept her if she could bear a son in the future.

Turning back to Naomi's persuading speech to her daughters-in-law and in light of the reason for sending Lanzhi home in the Chinese poem, we notice that Naomi emphasized her inability to bear sons because of her old age. Nobody can force an old woman to bear a child or blame her because she cannot give birth. It is a young girl's responsibility. But Naomi emphasized her responsibility of giving birth in front of her young daughters-in-law, who had not given birth for ten years. Although her tone was very humorous, she actually complained about her young daughters-in-law who could not bear grandsons for her, and who now left her alone in the world.

NAOMI'S FIRST SILENCE

The older daughter-in-law Orpah kissed Naomi and went back to her people and to her gods, but Ruth clung to her:

> "Do not press me to leave you or to turn back from following you! Where you go, I will go; where you lodge, I will lodge; your people shall be my people, and your God my God. Where you die, I will die—

---

[8] Daide, *Da Dai Li Ji* (Changsha: The Commercial Press, 1937), 220.
[9] This day is remembered as the cowherd and the weaving maid meeting each other across the Milky Way.

there will I be buried. May the Lord do thus and so to me, and more as
well, if even death parts me from you." When Naomi saw that she was
determined to go with her, she said no more to her. (Ruth 1:16–17)

This Moabite woman who at first believed Astarte and Chemosh (Num 21:29, Judg 11:24, 2 Kgs 3:27) was willing to follow Naomi and receive her God. She even took an oath, "if even death parts me from you." How did Naomi respond to such a commitment? She said no more to her daughter-in-law. Why did Naomi keep silent at this time? Generally speaking, "she was strengthening herself (מתאמצת—in effect, marshalling physical and mental resources. Faced with such determination, Naomi ceased to speak to Ruth and kept silent for the rest of the trip."[10] When we read the verses of Lanzhi's speech in the Chinese poem, we have new insight into Naomi's silence.

On the farewell day, Lanzhi arose early and got dressed. When she met her mother-in-law in the hall, she said the following:

> When I was a lass, I grew up in a place amid wild grass. Since I didn't receive much schooling there, I am a stigma to a noble heir. I've got from you more gifts than I can tell, but I've not been trained to serve you well. And today I'll have to leave your doors, I'm sorry you'll be burdened with the chores.[11]

Lanzhi's speech looks like she is reproaching herself, but in fact she was protesting. Her dressing and her words mentioned above show her dignity. By contrast, her mother-in-law shows pride and silence now, which in fact disguised her false reserve. Looking at Naomi's words in light of the words of Zhongqing's mother, Naomi complained about her daughters-in-law, because they did not bear grandsons for her. But now, Ruth, a Moabite widow, revealed the virtue of her character. This made Naomi feel regretful, so she kept silent. At the same time, Naomi was not sure if Ruth would keep her oath in the future, so she maintained her silence.

---

[10] BDB, 55; Ilona Rashkow, "Ruth: The Discourse of Power and the Power of Discourse," in *The Feminist Companion to Ruth*, ed. Athalya Brenner (Sheffield: Sheffield Academic Press, 1993), 32.
[11] Rongpei, *300 Early Chinese Poems*, 111.

Naomi's Second Speech

So Naomi returned with Ruth her daughter-in-law from the country of Moab and came to Bethlehem, and the whole town was stirred because of them:

> And the women said, "Is this Naomi?" She said to them, "Call me no longer Naomi, call me Mara, for the Almighty has dealt bitterly with me. I went away full, but the Lord has brought me back empty; why call me Naomi, when the Lord has dealt harshly with me, and the Almighty has brought calamity upon me?" (Ruth 1:19–21)

Although Naomi had nothing at this time, she still did not forget to laugh at the situation in hand, with her name. The meaning of Naomi (נעמי) is "pleasant, sweet," while Mara (מרא) means "bitter."[12] Such wordplay discloses the change in Naomi's fate. Commenting on "the LORD has brought me back empty," Athalya Brenner notes that since Naomi was accompanied by Ruth, Naomi was no longer empty. But Naomi does not mention Ruth in her speech.[13] Although Naomi was an elder, Brenner did not give her blind sympathy but persists with a neutral attitude. Zefira Gitay thought the reasons that Naomi only addressed the women in Bethlehem firstly was that she was worried about the social status of herself and her daughter-in-law. So when they entered the city, Naomi tried to forestall any harsh words her people might utter against them. Secondly, Naomi needed sympathy: she called for comfort and sought the support of her fellow people. However, Ruth was a threat to the women in Bethlehem; she was a Moabite and, by returning with Naomi, would have to be redeemed by a Judahite man. In such a case, Naomi avoided talking about Ruth.[14]

Considering again the Chinese poem, we suggested that Zhongqing's mother asked her son to dismiss his wife, because she did not like her. Lanzhi, the daughter-in-law, had no place in her heart despite years of marriage, and we can see a feudal mother-in-law's coldness and selfishness. Looking back at Naomi's second speech in the light of the Chinese poem, the word "empty" showed Naomi's inner heart. Even if Naomi said these words with no malicious intent, Ruth

---

[12] BDB, 653.
[13] Athalya Brenner, "Naomi and Ruth," in Brenner, *The Feminist Companion to Ruth*, 70–84.
[14] Zefira Gitay, "Ruth and the Women of Bethlehem," in Brenner, *The Feminist Companion to Ruth*, 82–183.

probably still felt guilty because she had borne no children. Naomi seemed more concerned about her own pain, without considering Ruth's feelings. If Naomi said these words intentionally, then Naomi was really not satisfied with Ruth her daughter-in-law. Ruth is omitted in Naomi's second speech, and Naomi did not receive Ruth in her heart until now. I think Brenner's explanation is more reasonable in light of such a cross-textual reading.

Naomi's Second Silence

So Boaz took Ruth, and she became his wife; then she bore him a son, Obed. The women of Bethlehem said to Naomi:

> "Blessed be the Lord, who has not left you this day without next-of-kin; and may his name be renowned in Israel! He shall be to you a restorer of life and a nourisher of your old age; for your daughter-in-law who loves you, who is more to you than seven sons, has borne him." Then Naomi took the child and laid him in her bosom, and became his nurse. (Ruth 4:14–16)

The women's approval at this moment contrasts sharply with their earlier ignorance. "Who is more to you than seven sons" indicates that the women in Bethlehem had completely received this Moabite woman.[15] Thus, Ruth's value for Naomi was clearly shown by these women's approval. How did Naomi respond to such high praise? She "took the child and laid him in her bosom" and kept silent again. Observing Naomi's former speech, we can see that she was a talkative woman, with first-rate language skills. But why did she keep silent at this moment when she should have spoken? We can compare the situation with Zhongqing's mother in the Chinese poem to find an explanation. Upon hearing that Lanzhi was forced to remarry the prefect's son, Zhongqing decided to bid farewell to his mother: "It is I who make this dismal plan, don't blame the gods, the ghosts or any man!" When the mother heard these words, her tears began to rain down in a flood: "Why die for a woman so inferior? She's unworthy of a man so superior." These two

---

[15] "In the ancient world it was believed that seven sons secured a man's well-being in the underworld. With no little irony, these women give the ultimate in praise to one daughter-in-law"; Adrien J. Bledstein, "Female Companionships: If the Book of Ruth Were Written by a Woman," in Brenner, *The Feminist Companion to Ruth*, 130.

words "inferior" and "superior" let us see clearly again that Zhongqing's mother is cold-blooded and selfish.

Looking back at the biblical text in light of Zhongqing's mother, it seems that Naomi should thank Ruth for this son, according to the women's words in Bethlehem. Amy-Jill Levine thinks that the marriage of Boaz and Ruth could erase the Moabite identity of Ruth.[16] Adrien J. Bledstein states that Naomi was "built up" through Ruth, as Rachel and Leah were through Bilhah and Zilpah.[17] But from the perspective of Naomi, could not Ruth do such a thing with her son in their marriage? This child was more a compensation than a gift to her, so Ruth is never more to her than her own sons. But she could not challenge the public opinion, so it is better for her to keep silent. Secondly, in her first speech Naomi complained about her daughters-in-law, because they did not bear grandsons for her in their ten years marriage, but now Ruth and Boaz, who was an old man (Ruth 3:10), had a son immediately. Generally speaking, ordinary people would guess that Ruth was fertile but Naomi's son was not. This would be shameful for Naomi and her sons. The women in Bethlehem certainly would compare Boaz to Naomi's sons. In order not to arouse rumors, it is better for her to keep silent.

Conclusion

In general, conflict between mother-in-law and daughter-in-law is common in societies deeply influenced by Confucian culture. This conflict is a ramification of a patriarchal society in which the rights of mothers-in-law are manifested.[18] Thus, mothers-in-law are spokespersons of patriarchal societies, and they in fact act as token men, helping men to manage women. Many Chinese literary works reflect such a conflict, the most famous being *A Pair of Peacocks to the Southeast Fly*.

In the Hebrew Bible, the book of Ruth is the only text that directly describes the relationship between mother-in-law and daughter-in-law. This chapter reread the relationship between Naomi and Ruth in the perspective of that of Zhongqing's mother and Liu Lanzhi and suggested that Naomi's two speeches and two silences imply her complaint to her daughters-in-law. We can see the figure of this difficult mother-in-law

---

[16] Levine, "Ruth," in *Women's Bible Commentary*, 90.
[17] Bledstein, "Female Companionships," 129.
[18] Lin Suqing, "Behind the Conflicts of Mother and Daughter-in-law: An Explanation on the Marriage Tragedy of A Pair of Peacocks to the Southeast Fly and Phoenix Hairpin," *Writer Magazine* 5 (2008): 153.

contrasted with Ruth's dedication. Ruth cannot surrogate Naomi's dead sons, and she does not receive the women's praise, "Who is more to you than seven sons" for Naomi. Such conflicts appeared in the families of ancient Israel also, not just in ancient China, so they are a common problem in any patriarchal society, although there are differences in degree.

A REINTERPRETATION OF LEVIRATE MARRIAGE IN RUTH 4:1–12 FOR KACHIN SOCIETY

Roi Nu

The term "levirate" is derived from the Latin word *"levir,"* meaning "brother-in-law." It occurs as יבם (*ybm*) in the Hebrew Bible, which as a noun is defined as a "husband's brother" and as a verb as "doing a brother-in-law's office."[1] When a man dies without leaving a son, the husband's brother takes the widow (his sister-in-law) as his wife and performs the *levir's* duty (Deut 25:5–10). This union is called levirate marriage. The main purpose of levirate marriage in the Hebrew Bible is "to raise up" the name of the dead and "to build up his house."[2] According to the Hebrew Bible, levirate marriage has been practiced from the time of the patriarchs (Gen 38).

The Kachins have been practicing some form of levirate marriage, called *karat hta ai*,[3] which means picking up a widow left behind by his brother. Among the Kachins, *karat hta ai* is a traditional practice and an unavoidable responsibility of the brother of the deceased. The Kachin tribe is an ethnic group in Myanmar constituting 2 percent of the total population (about 600,000); 99 percent of Kachin people are Christian.[4]

---

[1] Duane L. Christensen, *Deuteronomy 21:10–34:12*, WBC 6B (Nashville: Thomas Nelson Publishers, 2002), 606.
[2] Gerhard Von Rad, *Deuteronomy: A Commentary*, trans. Dorothea Barton (London: SCM, 1966), 154.
[3] Please see section one of the chapter, which describes the Kachin custom of *karat hta ai*. Leach and Tegenfeldt already used the term "levirate marriage" for the custom of *karat hta ai*. See Edmund R. Leach, *Political Systems of Highland Burma: A Study of Kachin Social Structure*, LSEMSA 44 (London: Athlone, 1954), 91, 140; and Herman Tegenfeldt, *A Century Growth: The Kachin Baptist Church of Burma* (South Pasadena, CA: The William Carey Library, 1913), 34. I use the Kachin term *karat hta ai* for levirate marriage in the whole article.
[4] The Kachins received the Gospel form American and Karen missionaries. The first American missionary was Albert J. Lyon (1878) and Karen missionaries were Bo Galey, Shwe Lin, and S' Peh, and Ko Teh. See Kachin Baptist Convention, "A

The Kachins are comprised of six subtribes: "Jinghpaw," "Atsi" (Zaiwa), "Maru" (Lawngwaw), "Rawang" (Nung), "Lashi" (Lachyik), and "Lisu" (Yawyin/ Lishaw). Every subtribe has its own dialect. The division of subgroups is based on linguistic diversity.[5] Even though they speak in different languages, they share the same ancestry, mythology, customs and rituals. I will use the term Kachin to refer to the whole Jinghpaw Wunpawng (Jinghpaw and its related peoples).

This chapter consists of three sections. The first section explains the Kachin custom of *karat hta ai*. The aim of this section is twofold: to introduce the custom of *karat hta ai* and its laws and to highlight its impact on Kachin society. The second section explores levirate marriage in the Hebrew Bible. In particular, I analyze the levirate marriage in Ruth 4:1–12. The third section reinterprets levirate marriage in the light of the Hebrew Bible for Kachin society. The implications of levirate marriage for Kachin society also will be described.

THE KACHIN CUSTOM OF *KARAT HTA AI*

Karat hta ai is a Kachin custom whereby a woman is married to a brother of her deceased husband. This is marriage within a family. The term *karat hta ai* as a noun means "picking up widow left by a brother." The word "karat" means "wife of an elder brother" and the meaning of "hta ai" is "picking up or rising up."[6] James George Scott reports that in the Kachin racial custom a widow is automatically taken by her husband's brother.[7] In Kachin tradition, picking up the widow left by the elder brother (*karat hta ai*) is considered a most important responsibility for a man and a very common practice. After the husband dies, the widow is usually forced to remarry her brother-in-law who is single or widowed or divorced. While some customs of the Kachin people vary according to geographical location, the custom and practices of *karat hta ai* remain consistent among the Kachin.

Short History and Formation of KBC," http://www.kbckachin.com/Page/KBC%20Bro.pdf.

[5] Ola Hanson, *The Kachin: Their Custom and Tradition* (New York: AMS Press, 1981), 13.

[6] The Kachin term *Karat* or *Rat* is using to call three different persons such as (1) a man to the wife of his elder brother, (2) a woman to younger brother of her husband, and (3) a man to elder sister of his wife.

[7] James George Scott, *Burma and Beyond* (London: Grayson, 1932), 176. Scott, an educated journalist, worked in Burma for London Evening Standard.

General Principles in the Custom of *Karat Hta Ai*

The law governing the custom of *karat hta ai* consists of two parts. The first part enforces the custom of *karat hta ai* on the widow to marry the deceased's brother or the nearest relative. The second part deals with the case where a widow refuses to fulfill the *karat hta ai* obligation. As Kachin society is patrilineal,[8] most relationships are reckoned from the male side. The first part of the law builds on the patrilineal concept, and bride price takes on an important role. The elements of Kachin customary law of *karat hta ai* are:

(1) After her husband dies, the widow is not allowed to return to her parents' house.
(2) The widow is forbidden to remarry a man of her choice. She remains at the disposal of her deceased husband's family.
(3) If she is young (young enough to produce children), she is generally married to a single or widowed or divorced brother-in-law or a cousin.
(4) The children from the *karat hta ai* shall take the name of the deceased brother.
(5) If no brother-in-law or cousin marries her, she may go back to her parents, but only after an agreement is reached between the two families. Her parents will return the bride price to her deceased husband's family.[9]
(6) If there is a brother-in-law to pick up the widow in the family and a man outside the deceased family wants to marry her, he has to give the bride price to the deceased family in the same measure that the deceased family had given. Moreover, he is obliged to take the family name of the deceased person and as well as the children from this union.[10]

---

[8] Tegenfeldt, *A Century Growth: The Kachin Baptist Church of Burma*, 24.
[9] Gilhodes, *The Kachins: Religion and Custom*, 2nd edition (New Delhi: Mittal, 1995), 227.
[10] Labang La Wawm, Interview. In this case, Pungga Ja Li presents a different view. He says that if a man outside the deceased family wants to marry a widow left by a deceased, he must take the family name of the deceased and there is no need to return any bride price to the deceased family. See Pungga Ja Li, *What Kachin Believe and Practice*, vol.1, 21. Labang La Wawm talks about a rule of *karat hta ai*, but Pungga Ja Li presents the application of today Kachin society to a rule

In the past, a widow has no right to refuse this marriage. In fact she may not even know about this decision before the marriage.[11] But nowadays, widows can refuse to marry her brother-in-law under certain exceptional circumstances.

First, if the appointed person (brother of the deceased husband or nearest relative) has a physical or mental disability, the widow can reject this marriage. Second, if she herself is no longer at child-bearing age and if she already has adult sons and daughters, she can refuse also.[12] In these situations, the widow can stay in her deceased husband's house without remarrying.

Third, if a widow is old and has only small children, one of her brothers-in-law may take care of her and his nephews and nieces and not take the widow as wife. Usually, he will support the children until they are able to fend for themselves.[13] If a widow rejects the union of *karat hta ai* without any good reason, she would remain in her deceased husband's house, and she would not be allowed to remarry outside the family.[14]

In the case of a Kachin Christian family, polygamy is not allowed,[15] and the married brother is automatically ruled out of consideration. But the next brother who is single is obliged to marry his deceased brother's wife. Maru Tang Gun describes the story of a close relative called Hpaumyang Tu. When Hpaumyang Tu was twenty years old, he got married to his *karat*. He is the youngest brother among his four siblings, and he married the widow of his oldest brother, because his two elder brothers were already married.[16] The elements of Kachin customary law of *karat hta ai* are built on the patrilineal concept of Kachin society, and its aims and purposes are intended to maintain the patriarchal status quo.

---

of *karat hta ai*. Pungga Ja Li's observation is based on the practice of Kachin society, and it show the principles in *karat hta ai* are more laxed in Kachin society today.

[11] Interview with N-Gan Tang Gun.
[12] Interview with Rev. Dr. Lahtaw Gum Se (May 2010).
[13] Gilhodes, *The Kachins: Religion and Custom*, 227.
[14] Interview with Maru Tang Gun (10 October 2010).
[15] During the pre-Christian period, polygamy was a common practice. The first wife is called Latung, the second Lashy, and the third Labai. Gilhodes, *The Kachins: Religion and Custom*, 225.
[16] Interview with Maru Tang Gun.

The Purposes of the Custom of *Karat Hta Ai*

The Kachin customary law of *karat hta ai* is threefold:

- The first purpose is survival of the family name of the deceased brother and maintaining family unity.
- Protecting widows is the second purpose. Basically the custom of *karat hta ai* presents a special concern for the widow of the deceased elder brother. The deceased family never abandons the widow. Their relatives with the same family name also regard themselves as responsible for her security and survival. The Kachin believe that the practice *karat hta ai* promotes the widow's dignity as a human being and provides her security in society.
- Preservation of family property within family is the third purpose of *karat hta ai*. Patrilineality as practiced by the Kachins does not regard women as worthy of inheriting either their parents' or their husbands' property.[17] Even though the widow can neither inherit nor take away her husband's property, she has a right to preserve it for a son who will be born to her brother-in-law.

In summary, the custom of *karat hta ai* represents an important social responsibility for the Kachins. It serves many purposes, such as survival of the family name, maintaining family unity, and protecting the widow left behind by a Kachin man. As Kachin society is patrilineal and patrilocal, the aims and basic principles of the custom of *karat hta ai* are reckoned from the male perspective. Kachin churches acknowledge the institution of *karat hta ai*. Although the custom of *karat hta ai* is not derived from the Bible, many Kachin churches think it is, which has led to confusion between culture and scripture. Undoubtedly, *karat hta ai* does have some resemblances with the Hebrew levirate marriage described in the book of Ruth and Deut 25:5–10 and so Kachin churches generally make the claim that the *karat hta ai* has biblical support. However, if studied more carefully, there are dissimilarities between the levirate marriage in the Hebrew Bible and the Kachin custom of *karat hta ai*. In the next part, I will deal with these texts.

---

[17] W. J. S. Carrapiett, *Kachin Tribes of Burma: For the information of Officers of the Burma Frontier Service* (Rangoon: Government Printing and Stationery, 1929), 98.

LEVITATE MARRIAGE IN RUTH 4:1–12

This section is an exegetical study of Ruth 4:1–12. After a word study on יבם, it argues that the marriage of Ruth and Boaz does not constitute levirate marriage.

A Word Study on יבם

The word יבם, meaning "brother-in-law," is a special term and seems to have an exclusive application in the Hebrew Bible for levirate marriage. יבם and its related forms occur only a few times in the contexts of brother-in-law or keeping a brother-in-law's duty.

יבם occurs as a noun as "brother-in-law" or "husband's brother" and occurs as a verb as "doing a brother-in-law's office" or "performing the duty of a brother-in-law."[18] We may understand from Deut 25:5–10 that the primary meaning of this denominative verb is doing the duty of יבם to the brother's widow in order to raise up a male heir to the deceased brother.[19] This duty is known as levirate marriage. The Hebrew Bible seems to infer levirate marriage in Gen 38, Deut 25:5–10, and probably Ruth 4.[20]

The root יבם occurs twice in noun (Deut 25:5, 7) and three times in verb (Gen 38:8, Deut 25:5, 7). The masculine noun of יבם is employed only in the Deut 25:5 passage to refer to the brother-in-law who is to perform the levirate duty.[21] The noun יבם has a feminine counterpart יבמה, "widowed sister-in-law," referring to a dead brother's widow (Gen 38:8, Deut 25:7, 9) or "sister-in-law" (Ruth 1:15). In the Hebrew Bible the noun יבם occurs only twice as a noun, but יבמה occurs five times (Deut 25:7a, b, 9; Ruth 1:15a, b).[22]

The verbal root יבם is only used in two contexts in the Hebrew Bible (Gen 38:8 and Deut 25:5, 7). Both occur in the piel stem. In Gen 38:8 the verb וְיַבֵּם ("to be levirate") is used by Judah to encourage his son, Onan,

---

[18] "יבם" in BDB, 386. The word levirate is derived from a Latin word *levir*, "brother-in-law." See Christensen, "Deuteronomy 21:10–34:12," WBC 6B, 606. Unfortunately, both the *levir* and levirate marriage is not mentioned in the Hebrew Bible. The Vulgate, the Latin Bible, also does not use the word *levir*, but *frater viri* or *frater eius* for brother-in-law (Deut 25:7b). See, E. Kutsch, "יבם ybm; יָבָם yābām; יְבָמָה yebāmâ," TDOT 5:370.

[19] Ralph H. Alexander, "יְבָמָה (yebēmâ) brother's wife, sister-in-law," TWOT, 836.
[20] Richard Kalmin, "Levirate Law" [Heb. *Yibûm*], ABD 4: 296–97.
[21] Alexander, "יְבֵמָה (yebēmâ) brother's wife, sister-in-law," TWOT, 836.
[22] Kutsch, "יבם ybm; יָבָם yābām; יְבָמָה yebāmâ," TDOT 5:368.

to perform the levirate duty. The word וְיִבְּמָהּ ("to be levirate") in Deut 25:5 and יַבְּמִי ("to be levirate") in Deut 25:7 are used to describe of the levirate legal law. In this context יבם is assigned to "consummate the marriage of a brother-in-law."[23] The piel of יבם, a denominative verb, is rendered "to do the duty of יבם to a brother's widow" and refers to a permanent marriage, not just the begetting of a son for the deceased brother. It means the widow becomes the woman or wife אשה ('iššâ) of her brother-in-law (Gen 38:14b, Deut 25:6).[24]

The root יבם "brother-in-law" is a special term for levirate duty, and it is directly related to levirate marriage. It is limited to the brother of the deceased man who is responsible for levirate duty. יבמה ("sister-in-law") is used more widely and outside levirate marriage. It is used in the meaning of "widowed sister-in-law" referring to a dead brother's widow (Gen 38:8, Deut 25:7, 9) and "sister-in-law" of a woman (Ruth 1:15) as well. With this study of יבם, now let me provide an exegesis of Ruth 4:1–2, the narrative text on the rite of levirate marriage.

An Exegesis of Ruth 4:1–12

Ruth 4:1–12 can be divided into two parts. The first part is "the negotiation of kinship ties"[25] among Boaz and the nearest kinsman. Boaz takes over the right of redeemer from the nearest kinsman (Ruth 4:1–6). The second part describes the ritual of removing the sandal (Ruth 4:7–12). My exegesis suggests the marriage of Ruth and Boaz is not a levirate marriage. Further, it will claim that the right that the next-of-kin transferred to Boaz is a redemption right. The key concept "next-of-kin," "redeemer," and "redemption right" appears frequently in Ruth 4 for rhetorical purpose.[26]

Calling of the Legal Session at the City Gate of Bethlehem (Ruth 4:1–2)

Having accepted the marriage proposal of Ruth at the threshing floor, Boaz becomes the main character of this story. He goes to the city gate of Bethlehem and addresses the next-of-kin to "come over here and sit down" and the next-of-kin sits with him (Ruth 4:1). The imperative סורה, meaning "turn aside" or "come over," expresses the authoritative

---

[23] William L. Holladay, "יבם" in *HALOT*, 126.
[24] Kutsch, "יבם ybm; יָבָם yābām; יְבָמָה yebāmâ," *TDOT* 5:368.
[25] Jack M. Sasson, *Ruth: A New Translation with a Philological Commentary and a Formalist Folklorist Interpretation* (Sheffield: JSOT Press, 1989), 104.
[26] Ibid, 198.

position of Boaz. Then he takes ten elders of the city to be witnesses and sits them down together (Ruth 4:2).

The Negotiation over Kinship Ties between Boaz and the Next-of-Kin (Ruth 4:3–6)

The negotiation of Boaz and next-of-kin begins with the words of Boaz. Boaz opens the negotiation for a piece of land, not Ruth's marriage proposal. In the presence of the elders and the people, Boaz offers a piece of land belonging to Naomi to the nearest kinsman to redeem it (Ruth 4:3). The nearest kinsman first accepts the field but then declines when Boaz informs him that this act also means he would acquire Ruth, the widow of Mahlon (Ruth 4:4–5). Finally, the "redeemer" (גאל, *go'el*) transferred his redemption right to Boaz. The word *go'el* appears in the meaning of nearest relative, translated next-of-kin and prescribed in Lev 25:24–34, 47–55.

In the Hebrew Bible, there are two usages of redeemer—a "figurative or religious" usage and a "secular or linguistic" usage.[27] In the figurative or religious usage, the redeemer is Yahweh. In the secular or linguistic usage, the term redeemer is used of a man's nearest relative or blood relative, and this is also the usage in family-law.[28] The redeemer refers to a man's brother, uncle, cousin, or some other kinsman (Lev 25:48). His major responsibility is to redeem and restore the relative's land and family possession (Lev 25:25–34, Jer 32:6) and slave if an Israelite sold himself to a foreigner as a slave (Lev 25:47–54). If the redeemer is not willing to redeem his relative, he can formally pass his responsibility to another kinsman in the presence of the elders at the city gate.[29] So, the *go'el* in the book of Ruth refers to a secular redeemer, the nearest kinsman of Elimelech. Boaz and the kinsman redeemer reach agreement and the kinsman redeemer transfers his redemption right to Boaz at the city gate of Bethlehem. What is transferred is not a levirate right but a redemption right. Four points support this.

First, the scripture text describes the right which the next-of-kin transferred to Boaz as the right of redemption. In Ruth 4:6, the next-of-kin says גאל־לך אתה את־גאלתי ("take my right of redemption yourself") to Boaz. Second, neither the nearest kinsman nor Boaz was a brother of Mahlon. The Bible does not describe the relationship of Boaz and the

---

[27] J.J. Stamm, "גאל g'l to redeem" in the *TLOT* 1:288.
[28] Holladay, "יָבָם," *HALOT*, 170.
[29] F. J. Taylor, "Redeem," in *Theological Wordbook of the Bible*, ed. Alan Richardson (New York: The Macmillan company, 1964), 186.

nearest kinsman to Elimelech. Deuteronomy 25:5 speaks of the limitation of levirate duty—it is the obligation of יבם ("brother-in-law") and יבמה ("sister-in-law"). The important key terms of levirate duty such as יבם ("brother-in-law") and יבמה ("sister-in-law") are not found in Ruth 4:1–12. The word אח ("brother") used in Ruth 4:3 to refer a male relative in general. In the Hebrew Bible, members of the same tribe or lineage are also called brothers (Num 16:10; 25:6; Judg 14:5). The Hebrew word אח frequently refers to relatives besides brothers, such as nephews or cousins (Gen 14:16; 29:15), fellow tribesmen (Gen 9:25), and fellow countrymen (Exod 2:11).[30] The phrase "the man is a relative of ours" in Ruth 2:20 also explains the relationship of Boaz to the family of Elimelech in a general sense. So, Boaz is regarded as a distant relative of Mahlon.

Third, the levirate duty is not transferable (Deut 25:5–10). Even though the *levir* can refuse the levirate duty by performing the sandal ceremony, he is not allowed to transfer his right of levirate to other relatives. The voluntary levirate duty on the part of distant relatives is not presupposed. Fourth, in Ruth 4:3 a piece of land unmentioned previously appears in the story suddenly. The mention of the land in Ruth 4:3 confirms that the right that the next-of-kin transferred to Boaz is the right to redeem the land of a relative, the primary duty of a kinsman redeemer. In some cases, especially marriage, "buy" or "acquire" refers to the changing of hands without immediate payment.[31] And Boaz makes no claim of actual price in this case. Therefore, the piece of land serves as proof that it is the redemption right which the next-of-kin transferred to Boaz.

The Custom of Taking off the Sandal (Ruth 4:7–8)

Ruth 4:7 is a comment of the narrator explaining the symbolic custom to be performed in Ruth 4:8. This explanation shows that the audience was not familiar with the custom. In Ruth 4:8, the next-of-kin transfers his right of redemption and takes off his sandal. Campbell comments that it is not obvious which custom was practiced in Ruth 4:7–8, with the most possible being that the kinsman redeemer gave Boaz his shoe, symbolizing the transfer of the redemption right.[32]

---

[30] BDB, 630.
[31] Cf. R.L. Hubbard, *The Book of Ruth* (Grand Rapids: Eerdmans, 1988), 244.
[32] Edward F. Campbell, *Ruth: A New Translation with Introduction, Notes and Commentary*, AB 7 (Garden City: Doubleday, 1975), 149–50.

The scripture clearly states that taking off a sandal was a custom to do with redeeming and exchanging in ancient Israel (Ruth 4:7). The next-of-kin took off his sandal himself and gave it to Boaz to serve as a symbol of exchanging the redemption right. No one removed his sandal. It is probable that the practice in Ruth 4:7– 8 is not a sandal removing ceremony but a symbolized transfer of redemption right.

To define the assembly at the city gate as a ceremony of removing the sandal that is related to levirate marriage is probably too far-fetched. According to the levirate law, the widow must make an announcement of the denial by her brother-in-law first, and only afterwards does the ritual of removing the sandal take place at the city gate (Deut 25:7). But in the book of Ruth the meeting at the city gate is called by Boaz, and there was no participation at all by Ruth. By levirate law, the widow of the deceased has the right to participate as a main character in the sandal removing ceremony. She shall pull off the *levir's* shoe, spit in his face, and announce some words (Deut 25: 7–9). In Ruth 4:7–8, there is no action by Ruth in the sandal removing ceremony; she was just waiting for the news in her house. So, the removing of the sandal of the kinsman redeemer is not conducted in accordance with levitate law in Deut 25:9–10. Taking off the sandal in Ruth 4:7–8 symbolized the transfer of the redemption right, and it also served as a symbol of refused responsibility and authority.

Some biblical scholars propose that the marriage of Boaz and Ruth is levirate marriage and the sandal ceremony in Ruth 4:7–8 serves as a positive reference in support. But the sandal removing ceremony itself demonstrates that the marriage between Ruth and Boaz is not levirate marriage as instituted in Deut 25:5–10.

The Witnessing by Elders and Blessing from the People (Ruth 4:9–10)

Witnessing is essential in order to make the transaction legal with the ancient jury of Israel. This is a legal formula used to notarize transactions contracted orally, and the elders and the people were notarizing the transactions being declared.[33] It seems there was no written record to be kept and people who gather along with the elders will stand to verify its legality for any future disputes. Boaz's right to act as redeemer was confirmed by the elders and the people announced the blessing. The people first bless Ruth, and then they also pray for the house of Boaz to be like the house of Perez (Ruth 4:12).

---

[33] Hubbard, *The Book of Ruth*, 254.

The rest of the chapter is a genealogy, but it is very important as it proves that the marriage between Ruth and Boaz is not a levirate marriage. Deuteronomy 25:6 clearly states that the first son from a levirate marriage shall succeed to the name of his brother who passed away and that the name of the deceased may not be blotted out of Israel. At the end of the book of Ruth, the genealogy of David is given. In that genealogy, the name of Mahlon and Elimelech are omitted.

Deuteronomy 25:5–10 emphasizes the ideal of perpetuating the name of the deceased as the main purpose behind levirate practice, and in Ruth the redemption of the land of Elimelech is the primary intention. Deuteronomy describes the law of levirate marriage, and Ruth 4:1–12 talks about the right and custom of redemption. Therefore, it is fair to say there is no concrete connection between Deut 25:5–10 and Ruth 4:1–12.

Levirate marriage or *karat hta ai* is one of the Kachin traditional marriage systems. Some Kachin pastors teach that levirate marriage is mandated by God and that Deut 25:5–10, and the book of Ruth support this interpretation. I have shown here that the custom narrated in the book of Ruth is in fact not levirate marriage; it is the custom of redemption. Therefore, the redemption custom in Ruth 4:1–12 should be reinterpreted for Kachin society. The task of reinterpretation in the light of Kachin traditions will be the subject of the next section.

A REINTERPRETATION OF LEVIRATE MARRIAGE IN RUTH 4:1–12 FOR KACHIN SOCIETY

The foregoing demonstrates that the marriage of Ruth to Boaz is not a levirate marriage but in accordance with the custom of redemption. It is similar to *hpunau gaida hta ai* in Kachin. This section reinterprets the levirate marriage in the Hebrew Bible for the benefit of Kachin society. From the Kachin perspective, the marriage between Ruth and Boaz in Ruth 4:1–12 could be understood according to the practice of *hpunau gaida hta ai,* "picking up the widow of a lineage brother." Boaz, who is not Ruth's brother-in-law but a distant relative to Mahlon, appeals to a practice similar to *hpunau gaida hta ai.* This section is divided into two parts. The first part is my attempt to reinterpret Ruth 4:1–12 for Kachin society. The second part applies this reinterpretation for the Kachin.

A Reinterpretation of the Marriage of Ruth and Boaz from the Kachin Perspective

From a Kachin perspective, Ruth 4:1–12 describes the custom of *hpunau gaida hta ai*. *Hpunau gaida* means "widow of a lineage brother," and *hta ai* means "picking up." Therefore, the term *hpunau gaida hta ai* as a noun means "picking up the widow of a lineage brother."[34]

Leach refers to the *hpunau gaida hta ai* in his book in this way: "if a man dies, his widow is collected by a lineage brother."[35] If the widow remains in her deceased husband's house for a few years and no brother of the deceased picks her up, a man from the same lineage of the deceased husband can marry her. For example, a widow of X can be married to Y, who is of the same lineage as X. For this kind of marriage, Y and his family do not need to provide a substantial bride price. Negotiation between the families of X and Y is essential. Y might go to the house of X with some elders, bringing a bag of sticky rice, rice wine, and some valuable things as a token of thanks. After negotiation, Y is recognized as a brother of X and he has the permission to marry the widow from the family of X. If Y is from a different subclan of X, Y does not need to take the clan name of X nor the children from of this union. However, for this type of arrangement, the widow reserves the right to refuse the proposal. If she does not want to marry him, she can refuse this marriage. *Hpunau gaida hta ai* requires the willingness of both participants. Even though Boaz did not go with the elders to see Naomi or the next-of-kin in ceremony, the marriage of Boaz and Ruth is quite similar to the *hpu nau gaida hta ai* of the Kachins. I will make three further points in support.

First, Boaz calls Elimelech אח ("brother"; Ruth 4:3). The word אח refers to a member of the same tribe or lineage brother (Num 16:10, 25:6, Judg 14:5). It also refers to a fellow tribesman (Gen 9:25) or fellow countryman (Exod 2:11) in the Hebrew Bible.[36] Thus, it is probable that

---

[34] Picking up the widow of a brother is a literal translation of *hpunau gaida hta ai*. *Hpunau gaida hta ai* is often confused with *karat hta ai* and *gaida hta ai*. As *karat hta ai* also involves picking up the widow of a deceased brother, it is sometimes considered as *hpunau gaida hta ai*. *Gaida hta ai* is an inclusive term and refers to any kind of picking up of widows, especially picking up widows outside the deceased husband's family and lineage as well.

[35] Leach, *Political System of Highland Burma: A Study of Kachin Social Structure*, 165. Leach uses the term "collecting a widow of deceased lineage brother."

[36] BDB, 630.

Boaz is a lineage brother of Elimelech and that the marriage of Boaz to Ruth is somewhat similar to *hpunau gaida hta ai* of the Kachins.

Second, in the custom of *hpunau gaida hta ai,* the one who picks up the widow of a lineage does not need to raise the family name or clan name of the deceased husband of the widow. The children of this union do not need to take the name of the deceased. The genealogy in Ruth 4:17–22 does not contain the name Mahlon or Elimelech, only Boaz. The offspring of Boaz also does not take the name of Mahlon. Therefore, the marriage of Ruth and Boaz is quite similar to the *hpunau gaida hta ai* of the Kachins.

Third, the *hpunau gaida hta ai* is not a strictly observed practice like the custom of *karat hta ai*. It has no stated rules and regulations. In actual practice, the *hpunau gaida hta ai* is a form of provision for the widow who has fallen in love with another man outside the family of deceased. The man may then initiate the *hpunau gaida hta ai* custom so that the family of the deceased can recognize him as one of their family members so that he may marry the widow. Therefore, *hpunau gaida hta ai* operates on the free will of the couple. Similarly in the story of Ruth, Ruth is willing to marry Boaz, and Ruth and Naomi choose Boaz rather than the next-of-kin. Moreover, Boaz initiates their marriage process. Hence, Boaz marries Ruth in accordance with *hpunau gaida hta ai,* "picking up widow of a lineage brother."

In Kachin tradition, all kinds of "picking up a widow" begins with the family of the deceased husband. If there is a suitable brother of the deceased to marry the widow, the custom of *karat hta ai* will be practiced. If there is no appropriate brother of the deceased, the levirate duty is extended to a cousin brother. If there is no cousin to marry the widow, a man from the same linage as the deceased will have priority to pick up the widow. If no brother or cousin or lineage brother of the deceased will pick her up, the widow is given free choice for her second marriage.

Possible Solution for Understanding *Karat Hta Ai* for the Kachins

Many Kachins consider *karat hta ai* as good custom for Kachin society, because it gives security to the life of widows and children left behind by the Kachin men. Since the practice has changed in different contexts, I will trace the evolution of the custom of *karat hta ai*.

In primitive times, the life of a Kachin man was full of danger, with many males dying in their adulthood. The young widow left behind by her husband was picked up by her brother-in-law in levirate marriage. The lineage and property of the deceased was sustained by his brother.

The widow came under the protection of the nearest relative, for a widow could not survive without the protection of a man at that time. So, the custom of *karat hta ai* represents a positive response to the social demand of ancient Kachin society. Until the early 1900s, when British colonialism began, the levirate duty extended to the father-in-law.[37] Nowadays, *karat hta ai* is limited to the brother-in-law or the cousin brother-in-law. Many Kachins think this represents progress of the custom of *karat hta ai*.

But such reasoning does not totally convince many Kachins, including me, because there is a dark side to the custom of *karat hta ai*. *Karat hta ai* degrades the dignity and freedom of widows, as well as the freedom of choice of the brother of the deceased. Hence, reform of the custom of *karat hta ai* is needed. I will describe some possible ways of dealing with *karat hta ai* for the Kachin society of today.

First, I propose to include a Kachin traditional meeting of refusal into the general principles of *karat hta ai*. The meeting of refusal for *karat hta ai* is a social demand of today's Kachin society. It is not a new idea. It is based on the legislation of levirate law in Deuteronomy, particularly Deut 25:9. I propose to follow the principle of Deut 25:5–10 and extend the right to refuse for the widow as well. In this way, the custom of *karat hta ai* becomes a duty but not a compulsory one. The widow and brother-in-law can accomplish their responsibility in love and kindness and not by force of legislation or social pressure. In this way, the custom of *karat hta ai* safeguards human dignity and freedom in Kachin society and is a positive response to the changes of modern Kachin society.

My second concern is promoting the right of the widow in the family. *Karat hta ai* is a product of the patriarchal social structure of the Kachins. Yet in its history, the practice was not without provisions in favor of the widow in the family, some which have been forgotten. We need to rediscover these hidden rules. In an article by Kumje Roi Ja, two rules are referred to which show concern for the widow.

(1) If a widow remains in the house of the deceased husband with her children, she has a right to obtain all the property of the deceased husband. But if she marries outside the deceased family she might lose it.

(2) If the widow has no children, she can take half of the property of her deceased husband and the rest will be kept by the deceased's parents.[38]

---

[37] Carrapiett, *Kachin Tribes of Burma: For the Information of Officers of the Burma Frontier Service*, 36.

[38] Kumje Roi Ja, "Jiwoi Jiwa Ni A Prat Kaw Nna Wunpawng Shayi Num Sha Ni Hpe Makawp Maga Da Ai Ahkaw Ahkang Ni," *Buga Shanan* 2005–2006.

The rules affirm the Kachin widow's right of inheritance of the deceased husband's property. But in many families the right of widows has been abused. Such rules about the rights of women have been neglected and forgotten. To rediscover and promote the rights of the widow in the Kachin family is crucial.

In a Kachin perspective, Ruth 4:1–12 describes the custom of *hpunau gaida hta ai* ("picking up widow of lineage brother") and not *karat hta ai*. Therefore, Ruth 4:1–12 no longer supports the claim of Kachin levirate marriage.

CONCLUSION

At the start of the chapter, I pointed out the origin of *karat hta ai* and how the teaching of the church has been that this custom is derived from the Hebrew Bible, in particular from Deut 25:5–10 and Ruth 4:1–12. I argued that *karat hta ai* in fact preexisted the Christian era of the Kachins and that it is based on the custom of cousin marriage instead. I also argued that Ruth 4:1–12 does not describe a levirate marriage; in fact, it describes the custom of redemption. I have also shown that the Kachin custom of *karat hta ai* is a far more strict practice than levirate marriage in the Hebrew Bible. This permits me to propose that the refusal law of levirate in Deut 25:5–10, namely, the meeting of refusal, can be and should be extended to Kachin society. I believe the practice in Ruth 4:1–12 is some kind of *hpunau gaida hta ai* ("picking up widow of lineage brother") of the Kachins. I also proposed to equip Kachin society with a new understanding of levirate marriage.

I do not claim that what I have done represents complete research on the custom of *karat hta ai*. This practice has some variations according to geography, and there may well be further data and understanding on this subject. However, I believe this study makes three contributions to Kachin society. First, I hope that my research will help Kachin society understand that the Kachin custom of *karat hta ai* is not a sacred law. It is purely a tradition, one which is no longer feasible. Second, I also hope that my study will encourage Kachin women to resist abuses, especially those related to *karat hta ai*. To appreciate the value and ability of women is more important than *karat hta ai* in Kachin society. Finally, I hope that my research will help readers to understand that the union depicted in

---

http://www.kachinnet.net/Article/2006/JanMarch/unpawng%20shayi%20num%20kasha%20ni%20hpe%20makawp%20maga%20da%20ai%20ahkaw%20ahkang.htm. The title of the article can be translated as "the rules which protect the Kachin women since primitive time."

Ruth is not the levirate marriage as prescribed in Deut 25:5–10. Hence, it should not be used to support the Kachin custom of *karat hta ai*.

An Intertextual Reading of Ruth and Proverbs 31:10–31, with a Chinese Woman's Perspective

Elaine W. F. Goh

The character description *'ēšet hayil* in Ruth 3:11 echoes Prov 31:10. This description invites various translations in both Ruth and Proverbs. Following this lead, this chapter opens up more correspondences between the two biblical texts through an intertextual reading. It focuses on the characterization of *'ēšet hayil* in Ruth as a person and in Prov 31:10–31 as the personified wisdom. This chapter will reflect on these questions: What accounts for an *'ēšet hayil*? How does *'ēšet hayil* contribute to our understanding of Ruth the Moabite and of Lady Wisdom? And how does *'ēšet hayil* relate the two biblical books?

The *'ēšet hayil* in the Book of Ruth

> And now, my daughter, do not be afraid. All that you have said, I will do to you. For all of my people in the town know that you are *a woman of strength*. (Ruth 3:11)[1]

The *'ēšet hayil* in Ruth 3:11 is a woman of certain attribute. The Revised Standard Version (RSV) and the New Revised Standard Version (NRSV) take it to mean a woman of worth. The New King James Version (NKJV) translates it as "a virtuous woman," and the New American Standard Bible (NASB) uses "a woman of excellence." Since Ruth was a widow when Boaz said this to her, the wife notion of the term *'ēšet* is ruled out in most translations. I suggest instead to take it as "a woman of strength." Since the Hebrew word *hayil* basically means "power" or "capacity" and denotes elsewhere a valiant military action (Num 24:18), "a woman of strength" appears to be a closer portrayal to the description of Ruth.

Boaz avows that Ruth is an *'ēšet hayil*. What did the term mean when Boaz used such a description? I suggest its meaning in three parts, where Ruth is seen as Boaz's equal, a survivor, and one who makes it against all

---

[1] English translations in this chapter are mine, unless otherwise stated.

odds. I will suggest further that Boaz had something in mind with regards to this description, given the circumstance they were in at the threshing floor.

Boaz's Equal

The term *'ēšet hayil* that denotes Ruth recalls the description of Boaz in Ruth 2:1, *'îš gibbôr hayil*. The latter could mean a man of great strength (physically), but also appropriately, a man of great wealth (economically) as Boaz appears in the whole book. A woman of strength in Ruth 3:11 juxtaposes with a man of great strength in Ruth 2:1. As such, Ruth is seen as Boaz's peer and an equal that suits to marry him.[2] Both of the terms are not identical in their meaning. Ruth has no wealth or social status to fit the description *hayil*, while *'îš gibbôr hayil* refers to Boaz's wealth and social status. The term *'ēšet hayil* appears to refer to Ruth's strength both physical and cerebral.

In term of physical strength, it is said that Ruth gleaned about an ephah of barley following Boaz's permission (Ruth 2:16–17). One cannot ascertain how much barley is denoted by an ephah, but thirty to fifty pounds seem likely.[3] Ruth actually takes home an extraordinary amount for one person to glean—grain for several weeks' consumption.[4] This tells of Ruth's physical strength to carry them home singlehandedly. Besides, in term of cerebral capability, Ruth is the one who drives the whole threshing floor episode. She has carefully crafted her speech and is thoughtful of the right timing to approach Boaz. Ruth even discerns the appropriate time to leave the scene early next morning. Besides, her intention is to seek future subsistence. Thus the term is remarkably appropriate for Ruth—a woman of strength. Boaz acknowledges that she is strong physically and mentally.

---

[2] Robert L. Hubbard Jr., *The Book of Ruth*, NICOT (Grand Rapids: Eerdmans, 1988), 216.

[3] Tod Linafelt and Timothy K. Beal, *Ruth and Esther*, ed. David W. Cotter, Berit Olam Studies in Hebrew Narrative and Poetry (Collegeville, MN: Liturgical Press, 1999), 40.

[4] Linafelt and Beal, *Ruth and Esther*, 40. See also Jack M. Sassoon, *Ruth: A New Translation with a Philological Commentary and a Formalist-Folklorist Interpretation*, 2nd edition (Sheffield: Sheffield Academic, 1989), 55. The estimation is based on a reconstructed system of weights and measures in the ancient Near East.

A Survivor

Naomi initiates the whole episode on the threshing floor, and Ruth carries it out. She acts on a daring plan to lie at Boaz's feet. After being identified by him, she proposes marriage by asking Boaz to "spread his covering over her" (Ruth 3:9). The text does not indicate that Ruth's concern on the threshing floor is for Naomi's welfare, much less would Boaz reason as such when he saw Ruth to be an *'ēšet hayil*. Ruth's moral character appears to be out of the question. The scene is sexually suggestive, at Ruth's initiative. This circumstance calls Ruth's moral character into question, rather than affirming it as some have suggested.[5]

In this regard, Ruth's action is risky on three counts. First, her initiative recalls the one by Lot's older daughter that gave birth to Ruth's Moabite lineage (Gen 19:30–37). It recaps nothing else but a disgraceful past. Second, the possibility of her being rejected and, hence humiliated, is real. Boaz's pleasing of her in Ruth 2:11–12 ascertains his acceptance of her initiative. Third, Ruth could not ensure what would happen after the night. What if Boaz, after yielding to her seduction, has only one-night-pleasure in mind without committing to marriage? As Katharine Sakenfeld has pointed out, Boaz could have easily taken advantage of her physically.[6] So, what drives Ruth's risky actions? I suggest that it is driven by a survival need. Because of her survival instinct, Ruth is brave to make this move. Boaz could have picked up this risky consideration of Ruth, yielding to his acknowledgment of her as an *'ēšet hayil*—a woman of strength. Ruth does not give up on her misfortune. Boaz sees a woman who has a strong will to secure a future, even at the expense of her own dignity.

Against All Odds

Boaz affirms Ruth's virtue in Ruth 2:11. He has heard that Ruth followed her mother-in-law to a foreign land to call it home. In so doing, Ruth overcame cultural barriers and psychological obstacles. She might also have brought with her the bereavement of her dead husband and the painful reality that she nevertheless has to go on in life. There was so much uncertainty and so little to hold on to. Yet later, the report on Ruth in town implies a public acceptance of her—a Moabite in an Israelite

---

[5] For example, Hubbard, *Ruth*, 216–17.
[6] Katharine Doob Sakenfeld, *Ruth*, Interpretation: A Bible Commentary for Teaching and Preaching (Louisville: John Knox, 1999), 62.

town. For Boaz, it is remarkable for Ruth to have gone thus far. As readers, we know later that Ruth proceeds to become the wife of someone influential in Israelite society and gives birth to an ancestor of King David. Ruth does that against all odds. Her character narrates of something impossible made possible.

Given the sexually suggestive circumstance that they were in at the threshing floor, one wonders if Boaz and Ruth were sexually involved that night. A younger person could have succumbed to a lustful romance without a thought of commitment and responsibility that entails. Yet Boaz has a plan beyond one night's romance. He is mature enough to call Ruth "my daughter" (twice, in Ruth 3:10 and Ruth 3:11), and he praises Ruth for not having followed younger men (Ruth 3:11). Boaz is not only wealthy but is also upright: he fears God, and he is admired in the community.[7] He acknowledges that Ruth is his equal and that she has tried remarkably hard to survive. I suggest here that Boaz, being convinced that Ruth is assertive to what she wants, has determined to achieve what he wants.

Boaz picks up Ruth's terminology of next-of-kin in Ruth 3:9 and considers a larger implication of Ruth's expectation. He instructs Ruth to "lodge" the night and to "lie down till morning" (Ruth 3:13). His employment of the word "lodge" foresees Ruth's lodging with him after their marriage.[8] Besides, he asks her to spend the rest of the night with him by just lying down—"going to sleep." Boaz's plan is obviously not to satisfy a night's sexual urge. He is going to draw out a bigger plan the next day. In so doing, Boaz makes himself available for Ruth's against-all-odds sequel. Of course, his liking of her represents a determining factor for such commitment.

Reading Ruth 3:11 From A Chinese Woman's Perspective

I often wonder how to convey Ruth's narrative in Chinese women's circles. Ruth is largely perceived to be faithful and diligent, except for the threshing floor chapter. One may wonder how soon Boaz has arrived at her attention, when generally people still expect Ruth to be grieving. Many can easily identify with Ruth's concern for survival, but not many would condone her way of ensuring it. Fundamentally conservative, people nurtured in Chinese culture look upon any coquettish women negatively. Therefore, at the threshing floor Ruth could be easily deemed a crafty seductress. As a result, the label $'ēšet\ hayil$ is viewed as nothing

---

[7] Ibid, 63.
[8] Ibid, 64.

but a strong-willed, self-serving, guileful woman. Hence the interpretation of "a woman of worth" (NRSV) or "a virtuous woman" (NKJV) will be certainly ruled out. Nevertheless, the reading of *'ēšet hayil* as "a woman of strength" as I suggest is still valid. In other words, *'ēšet hayil* as "a woman of strength" has a cultural perspective in my reading. A woman who aspires to survive, albeit by shrewdness, is still a tough woman. Similar Chinese women of strength were identified throughout history and even at present. They ensure that households run smoothly, that stomachs are filled, and that the future is secured. Ruth possesses this strength.

THE *'ĒŠET HAYIL* IN PROV 31:10–31

A woman of strength who can find? She is far more precious than jewels. (Prov 31:10)

Proverbs 31:10–31 is an alphabetical poem, corresponding to the twenty-two characters of the Hebrew alphabet, singing praises of "a woman of strength." The *'ēšet hayil* in Prov 31:10–31 is a composite of various admirable traits. As its alphabetical sequence suggests, *'ēšet hayil* encapsulates everything from the beginning to the end. This acrostic poem represents one of the rare biblical passages that communicates women's mandate over many aspects of life. Unlike the one in Ruth, the *'ēšet hayil* in Prov 31:10 is widely taken as a "wife" in view of her family role in Prov 31:10–31. In all, the term highly suggests the "ideal wife" that is consistent in wisdom literature. The phrase *'ēšet hayil* also occurs in Prov 12:4: "A woman of strength is the crown of her husband, but she who brings shame is like rottenness in his bones." Like Prov 31:10–31, the *'ēšet hayil* in Prov 12:4 is set in the perspective of a wife in view of "her husband" in the text.

A variety of translations are suggested for *'ēšet hayil* in Prov 31:10, implying the many facets of its interpretations. To name only some, *'ēšet hayil* is "a capable wife (NRSV)," "a virtuous woman (KJV)," "an excellent wife (NASB)," "the woman of worth,"[9] "the Valiant Wife,"[10]

---

[9] Leo G. Perdue, *Proverbs*. Interpretation: A Bible Commentary for Teaching and Preaching (Louisville: John Knox, 2000), 275.
[10] Bruce K. Waltke, *The Book of Proverbs: Chapters 15-31*, ed. R. K. Harrison and Robert L. Hubbard Jr., NICOT (Grand Rapids: Eerdmans, 2005), 510–36.

"wife of noble character,"[11] "the woman of substance,"[12] and the like. The Hebrew word *hayil* basically means "power" or "capacity," and it recurs in Prov 31:17 and 31:25 as physical strength (as in Prov 31:3). Hence "a woman of strength" explains the verses that follow: she is strong, self-assured, independent, diligent, purposeful, and resourceful. One grasps from the entire poem the depiction of a versatile woman.

First, it begins with an introduction of *her value* in Prov 31:10–12 where her worth is due to her scarcity (Prov 31:10) and in relation to her husband (Prov 31:11–12). Second, Prov 31:13–27 encapsulates *her activities* essentially related to the household: her home industry (Prov 31:13–19) and her social achievements (Prov 31:20–27). Third, the poem concludes with *her praise* (Prov 31:28–31): by her family (Prov 31:28–29) and by all (Prov 31:30–31).[13] Her extraordinary description is presented in a superlative term as "surpassing all others (Prov 31:29)."[14] As a result of the acrostic construction of the poem, the content of the passage appears haphazard and disorganized.[15] Yet its unified theme of wisdom leads many readers to value it as proverbs, a song of praise, a wisdom psalm and even a "heroic hymn."[16]

A Socioeconomic and Cultural Reading

In this section, I offer a socioeconomic and cultural reading of the passage by reconstructing the world of ancient Israelite women. I also present a reading of the passage from a Chinese woman's perspective, then conclude with a personified Wisdom reading. In all, I employ a hermeneutic of consent to the portrait of the woman of strength, against the feminist objection that the image could affirm the male imagination

---

[11] Roland E. Murphy and Elizabeth Huwiler, *Proverbs, Ecclesiastes, Song of Songs,* New International Biblical Commentary (Peabody, MA: Hendrickson Publishers, 1999), 154–56.
[12] Christine Roy Yoder, "The Woman of Substance: A Socioeconomic Reading of Proverbs 31:10–31," *JBL* 122 (2003): 427.
[13] I am indebted to Waltke in this insightful structure of thoughts in his work, *Proverbs*, 515.
[14] Tom R. Hawkins, "The Wife of Noble Character in Proverbs 31:10–31," *Bibliotheca Sacra* 153 (1996): 12.
[15] For instance, the money used to buy the vineyard in v. 16 may originate from the sale of the clothing noted in v. 24; the spinning action in v. 19 comes after her manufacture of cloth in v. 13.
[16] Albert M. Wolters, "Proverbs 31:10–31 as Heroic Hymn: a Form-Critical Analysis," *VT* 38 (1988), 447.

and perpetuate stereotypes of female.[17] More importantly, the interpretation of feminine personified Wisdom is upheld, because it provides a remarkable conclusion to the book of Proverbs, which opens with Lady Wisdom in chapters 1–9 and closes with the same in chapter 31.

Reading Proverbs 31:10–31 in the Ancient Israelite Setting

Archaeological information helps to reconstruct the household of ancient Israelites, which was the primary locus of activities, particularly for women. Located in an agricultural background, women worked hard out on the field as well as domestically. They contributed to the production of food and clothing besides daily childcare and home education.[18] The numerous activities in carrying out this life-supporting system makes one amazed at the managerial responsibilities and household authority a woman had.[19] The degree of expertise and experience involved are also remarkable. Proverbs 31:10–31 depicts such a social situation of women that most likely reflects the pre-monarchic Israelite society. It is moreover employed in a postexilic text in search for a valid cultural model.[20]

---

[17] Katharine Doob Sakenfeld, *Just Wives? Stories of Power and Survival in the Old Testament and Today* (Louisville: Westminster John Knox, 2003), 129, points out the feminist objection with respect to the images of wisdom and folly in Proverbs as a whole, that the portrait of a woman in Prov 31 carries the danger of reinforcing the stereotypical female gender alternatives that leave little space for real and ordinary women.
[18] Carol L. Meyers, "Everyday Life: Women in the Period of the Hebrew Bible," in *Women's Bible Commentary*, ed. Carol A. Newsom and Sharon H. Ringe (Louisville: Westminster John Knox, 1992), 253.
[19] Meyers, "Everyday Life," 254–56.
[20] Ellen Louise Lyons, "A Note on Proverbs 31:10–31," in *The Listening Heart: Essays in Wisdom and the Psalms in Honor of Roland E. Murphy*, ed. Kenneth G. Hoglund et. al. (Sheffield: JSOT Press, 1987), 238, 241–42. In both premonarchic and postexilic periods, the roles and contributions of women were valued highly due to the required social energy to activate the subsistence activities. See also Perdue, *Proverbs*, 275.

She is a Household Manager

Claudia Camp points out the common expectation that a wife is to manage her household as portrayed in Prov 31:10–31.[21] In this poem, she is pictured as one who organizes and oversees all the needs of her household: purchasing, craft-making, selling, planting of fields, and the like. The readers can hardly escape the enormous tasks she manages. The many ventures she well engages undoubtedly makes her "far more precious than jewels" (v. 10). As the poem indicates, the woman has great authority.[22] The degree of such dominion evidently assumed that she was the wife of a wealthy man in ancient Israel. There is a loose connection that can be found in Abigail, the wife of Nabal in 1 Sam 25.

She is an Entrepreneur

The woman of strength in the poem endeavors with foresight in business dealings. She prepares raw material (v. 13), plans ahead (v. 14), delegates her work (v. 15), buys a piece of land and operates a vineyard (v. 16), earns profit (v. 18) and sells her home-made clothing (v. 24). She involves herself in the production that ensures the subsistence of her entire household (vv. 15, 19, 21). Given a modern scenario, the *'ēšet hayil* can be likened to an entrepreneur who is well versed in the delegation of tasks, the distribution of resources, and who has a good sense of trading.

She is a Teacher

"She opens her mouth with wisdom, and teaching of kindness is on her tongue" (Proverbs 31:26). The woman of strength resumes the duty of a teacher who imparts wisdom of the sages, the know-how to work on the field, the proper use of language, and the law of kindness to others.[23] This home-school education could go beyond to include social customs, moral values, and religious belief.[24] When she speaks, presumably when she teaches also, it is with wisdom and *ḥesed* (v. 26).

---

[21] Claudia V. Camp, *Wisdom and the Feminine in the Book of Proverbs* (Sheffield: JSOT Press, 1985), 85.

[22] Perdue, *Proverbs*, 276. The mother of Micah in Judges 17:1–4 was a woman of such comparable description. The passage speaks of her, presumably widowed, was wealthy and appeared to exercise dominion in the household. See Lyons, "A Note on Proverbs 31:10–31," 240.

[23] Perdue, *Proverbs*, 279.

[24] Ibid.

Her Dynamics with Her Husband

Kathleen O' Connor has wisely pointed out that the praise and honor lavished upon her by her husband and children (vv. 11–12, 28) do not come from her marriage to him but from the wisdom inherent in her behavior.[25] The poem does not elaborate on the husband's talents or activities in her involvement in the household. The impression of his position of honor and recognition is given instead in verse 23 where he sits among the elders at the city gate, signifying his influence and adjudicator role. His honorable role, however, appears secondary compared to his wife—who is the protagonist in the poem. There is irony here. The competent wife gives her husband an honorable household (one without domestic worries), and this results in his honorable position in the public life. But she is so honorably portrayed that the husband is almost driven out of picture.

While the woman of strength may not necessarily refer to a specific person, the passage depicts a typical diligent woman tied to a historical context.[26] She is located in a household where the economic functions determine its survival. The endeavors of the *'ēšet hayil* dominate the entire sphere of activities. Her strength is largely defined in terms of economic productivity, yet the poem affirms also her strong moral and intellectual capabilities.[27] She appears to be self-sufficient, rather resourceful, intelligent, and compassionate. The passage has a striking effect: the wife is not portrayed simply as the maintainer of the household but the source of its identity.[28]

---

[25] Kathleen A. Farmer, *Who Knows What Is Good? A Commentary on the Books of Proverbs and Ecclesiastes* (Grand Rapids: Eerdmans, 1991), 78.
[26] Yoder, "Woman of Substance," 427–47, suggests that a Persian bride is the female character depicted in Prov 31:10–31. Therefore, Yoder objects to the idea of a personified Wisdom reading.
[27] William McKane, *Proverbs: A New Approach* (Philadelphia: Westminster Press, 1970), 669. See also Camp, *Wisdom and the Feminine*, 91.
[28] Camp, *Wisdom and the Feminine*, 92. According to Camp, Prov 31 indicates the proper identity of the home where one finds its bearing in family life.

Reading Proverbs 31:10–31 from a Chinese Woman's Perspective

A Glimpse of a Patriarchal Society

One's experience shapes the way one reads the Bible.[29] The *'ēšet hayil* and ancient Chinese women have the same social organization and household experiences. The Chinese household is usually a patriarchal one. It was the basic social institution among ancient Chinese women. This cultural characteristic was deeply rooted in Chinese history mainly due to Confucius' teaching: family harmony impacts greater social well-being.[30] In the ancient world, many Chinese families operated housebound production. It required the interdependence of household members and working together for common subsistence. This participative principle concurs with the depiction of the *'ēšet hayil* in Proverbs. It is a model of energetic production in any household.[31]

Under such society however, the work that was executed by men in the public realm was more prized than that performed by women at home. A Chinese idiom, "men command the outdoor spheres whereas women, indoor," speaks volumes for itself. Proverbs 31:10–31 recollects a common traditional Chinese woman who is expected to be diligent and strong. But the passage had also been used to expect women to be bound at home. It should not necessarily be so these days. Instead, the passage represents an affirmation that women have multifaceted capabilities, even though women put the interests of her family closely at heart. Therefore, the poem upholds the strength and competence of women. Nevertheless, this does not necessitate marriage, childbirth, and wealth.

Modernization has revised the appreciation of the values of Chinese *'ēšet hayil*. A modern career woman who is both a mother and a wife would be proud to display such "strength." More and more Chinese women in developing countries are working mothers. It is common to employ foreign maids to do household chores and to "takeover" childcare. For career women, rather than discarding the passage of the

---

[29] Madipoane Masenya, "Proverbs 31:10–31 in a South African Context: A Reading for the Liberation of African (Northern Sotho) Women," *Semeia* 78 (1997): 56.

[30] The focal point of Confucius teaching aims at family harmony in particular and society well-being in general. The teaching of Confucius had direct impact on ancient Chinese society where households and family represent the center of activities for women.

[31] See also Ellen F. Davis, *Proverbs, Ecclesiastes, and the Song of Songs* (Louisville: Westminster John Knox, 2000), 151.

'ēšet hayil as a harsh yardstick, they are instead reminded of their priority and responsibilities for the well-being of their family. The Chinese people principally comprise a communal society whose honor is related to the success of maintaining a functional and healthy household. Chinese women likewise can exemplify wisdom in their lives by proper alignment of values, even though they gain in the process of modernization.

Toward "a Woman of Strength" Today

Chinese Christians recite Prov 31:10–31 on Mother's Day. Brides-to-be are also inclined to read the passage repeatedly. Many women are expected to possess similar qualities that the 'ēšet hayil possesses. Yet, the description is difficult to be met by any real woman. The rhetorical question "who can find?" (v. 10) in the beginning of the poem anticipates a negative answer: no one.[32] Even the closest biblical parallel, Ruth, hardly comes with total resemblance to Prov 31:10–31. Thus, one should avoid imposing unrealistic measurements on oneself or on another to avoid unnecessary stresses and disappointments.

Katharine Sakenfeld rightly pointed out a life-giving direction: Proverbs 31:10–31 is best used as "a conversation opener" about how one understands her own identity rather than as prescription to be emulated or discarded.[33] The female figures in the passage are not just literary forms. The author intended the readers to capture the picture of a capable, independent, resourceful, and diligent woman in a sociohistorical setting. Reading the poem as a wife and mother then, the woman of strength is indeed a model. Anyone whose character, commitment, godliness, and productivity reflect the qualities of this woman indeed lives wisely.

Notably, the poem does not praise the outlook of the 'ēšet hayil but indicates instead the deceitfulness of charm and vanity of beauty (31:30). In the modern world where women's purchasing power accelerates to lavish upon promoting good looks, one discovers in Prov 31:10–31 instead the strength and virtue of a woman who fears the LORD. Such strength is worth pursuing. It is prized more than the perishable qualities of outward charm and physical beauty.

---

[32] Roland E. Murphy, *Proverbs*, ed. Bruce M. Metzger et.al., World Biblical Commentary (Nashville: Thomas Nelson, 1998), 246. See also Kathleen M. O' Connor, *The Wisdom Literature* (Collegeville: Liturgical Press, 1988), 78.
[33] Sakenfeld, *Just Wives?* 127.

The Personified Wisdom Reading

There is "a universal type of wisdom" in addition to the portrait of the female figure in Prov 31.[34] In agreement with a handful of scholars, this paper sustains that the intentionally one-sided portrait of the woman is at the same time meant to have a symbolic meaning to Wisdom.[35] McCreesh's analysis of the poem's chiastic structure, its choice of words (repetition of "palm," "hand," "send," "strength" and "praise"), and the stylistic phrases ("who can find?") is largely persuasive for this symbolic interpretation.[36] The verb "find" means more than a casual finding. It has to do with "acquiring wisdom" (as of Prov 1:28 and 8:35).[37] It promotes the idea of wisdom as the finest attainable goal to cope more effectively in life.[38] The central question is, "where can one find 'Wisdom'?" One expects the answer: "nowhere, except with God!"[39] Hence, the rhetorical question in Prov 31:10 appears to be a riddle suggesting that Lady Wisdom is not only incomparable, but her identity is to be discovered.[40] Therefore when one pursues Wisdom, one finds God.

Reading *'ēšet hayil* as "Wisdom Incarnate" in Prov 31:10–31, one discerns the deliberate *inclusio* in Prov 1–9 and Prov 31.[41] The point of the *inclusio* is to craft the significance of wisdom. As a summary, the concluding acrostic poem characterizes a familiar "hymnic *halleluyah*" in the Psalter.[42] Thus, in the book of Proverbs, from beginning to end, Wisdom appears as a feminine character grounded in the sapiential emphasis on the fear of the LORD.[43] Lady Wisdom hence stands in stark contrast to the feminine depiction of foolishness in Proverbs.

---

[34] Camp, *Wisdom and the Feminine*, 93.
[35] See for example, Thomas P. McCreesh, "Wisdom as Wife: Proverbs 31: 10–31," *Revue Biblique* 92 (1985): 28; Naphtali Gutstein, "Proverbs 31:10–31: The Woman of Valor as Allegory," *Jewish Bible Quarterly* 27 (1999): 36–39; and Tom R. Hawkins, "The Wife of Noble Character in Proverbs 31:10–31," *Bibliotheca Sacra* 153 no 609 (1996): 12–23.
[36] McCreesh, "Wisdom as Wife," 31–35.
[37] Murphy, *Proverbs*, 246.
[38] Gustein, "Proverbs 31:10–31," 36–37.
[39] McCreesh, "Wisdom as Wife," 37.
[40] Ibid, 38.
[41] Gustein, "Proverbs 31:10–31," 38. See also Farmer, *Who Knows What is Good?* 127.
[42] It relates to the summons of Lady Wisdom in 9:4–6, inviting guests to her home in chapter 9, and finally settling down with her own in chapter 31. McCreesh, "Wisdom as Wife," 25, 46. See also Wolters, "Heroic Hymn," 450.
[43] Murphy, *Proverbs*, 249–50.

In short, the Israelite image of *'ēšet hayil* is communicable with the experience of Chinese women, and the image should continue to be upheld as an ongoing dialogue between the biblical world and our practical life. In reality we do have multitalented women endowed with many capabilities, yet the description of the *'ēšet hayil* embodies "a woman of vast experience and *the wisdom* that such experience brought."[44] More importantly, personified wisdom is conveyed through the portrayal of this resourceful and diligent woman. Such wisdom is worth grasping, as much as the woman of strength is worth pursuing.

Intertexting the *'ēšet hayil* in Ruth and Proverbs

The phrase *'ēšet hayil* appears in both Ruth 3:11 and Prov 31:10. The phrase connects both passages. Their contexts are set in exaltations for a particular woman: Ruth and Lady Wisdom, respectively. Sakenfeld points out the second expression in Ruth that strengthens their intertextual connection.[45] It is literally "all the gate of my people" in Ruth 3:11. This expression recaps the concluding phrase from Prov 31:10–31, "Let her works praise her in the city gates" (Prov 31:31). Sakenfeld suggests that, as Boaz's wife, Ruth has become the embodiment of the woman of strength in Prov 31:10–31.[46]

Although these terms communicate something in common for the two passages, the protagonist described in Ruth and Proverbs have remarkable differences. I identify their resemblances first, then their contrasts.

Diligence

The *'ēšet hayil* in Ruth and Proverbs are related by their diligence. Ruth takes initiatives outside the household to provide for her family. Ruth goes to the field and gleans the ears of grain behind the reapers (Ruth 2:2, 7). Ruth 2:17–18 tells us about her gleaning in the field until evening. There she gleans a remarkable amount of barley in one day. Together with the bread and parched grain she saved earlier, she takes them home for Naomi. The produce she brought home will satisfy both of them for several weeks following.

---

[44] Lyons, "A Note on Proverbs 31:10–31," 240. Emphasis mine.
[45] Sakenfeld, *Ruth*, 62.
[46] Ibid.

Proverbs 31:10–31 encapsulates the activities of an *'ēšet hayil* that are essentially related to her household. She is actively involved in home industry. Like Ruth, she works with willing hands (Prov 31:13) and provides food for her household (Prov 31:15). In short, she does not eat the bread of idleness (Prov 31:27). Therefore, the "woman of strength" seems to communicate something about being industrious. Ruth's narrative, however, focuses more on her becoming Boaz's wife, rather than her diligence. Even her hard work in the field is designed by the author so that she may meet Boaz. So in Prov 31:10–31, diligence is the primary impression of *'ēšet hayil*, whereas in Ruth 3, diligence is secondary.

Marriage and Family

As maintained earlier, *'ēšet hayil* is "woman of strength." The meaning of *hayil* is essentially about forte, or might. Both Ruth and personified Wisdom are strong ladies. Nevertheless, while Ruth is not married with children at that point, the "woman of strength" in Proverbs is summed up in the context of her children and a husband. Further, *'ēšet hayil* in Ruth's narrative is found in the field, but in Proverbs she is mainly described in her household. Thus marriage and family are presupposed in Prov 31:10–31, but not in Ruth. As a result, in terms of marriage and family, Ruth differs significantly from the wife in Proverbs.

Conversely, this also communicates that *'ēšet hayil* is not defined strictly by a wife's or a mother's role. In the case of Prov 31:10–31 therefore, *'ēšet hayil* should not be used strictly for married women only. A single lady who is capable and versatile suits the title as well. So we too see *'ēšet hayil* today as a business woman, teacher, financial planner, manager, property supervisor, and the like—who is not necessarily married. Therefore, as an idea from this intertextual reading, I appropriate Prov 31:10–31 in a new setting. The poem could sing praises of a working woman who is capable and versatile and not necessarily married or with children. In reality, we find many of these competent women around us. They may be widows, single ladies, or single mothers; and they are capable women.

Social Standing

Apart from female characterization of Ruth and of Personified Wisdom, their social locations differ. While Prov 31:10–31 presumes an affluent household, Ruth is certainly not wealthy. She is a widow who can easily be deprived of economic advantages. This is notably true given that she is a foreigner in an Israelite town. She merely survives by garnering grains. The title therefore has nothing to do with social background. It rules out affluence as a criterion. This again affirms the reason why *'ēšet hayil* should be read as "a woman of strength." Further, it suggests that the competence of the protagonist in Prov 31:10–31 is more prominent than her wealth. In a nutshell, the *'ēšet hayil* in Proverbs and Ruth do not have equal social standing.

In short, *'ēšet hayil* in Proverbs fits Ruth appropriately, yet not entirely. Conversely, *'ēšet hayil* in Ruth reflect merely a part of what is characterized in personified Wisdom. Even though the phrase has similar basic assumptions, it encapsulates different meanings in Ruth and Proverbs. As Sakenfeld also points out, many key traits of "a woman of strength" are quite apart from the context of marriage, children, and wealth presupposed in Proverbs.[47] The disparities between them warn us the danger of rigid application of two different biblical texts. The term *'ēšet hayil* should have a contextual consideration. In so doing, Ruth's story can serve as a balance and a corrective to the assumption in Proverbs that a woman's worth is defined by marriage, offspring, and wealth.[48]

Conclusion

The *'ēšet hayil* in Ruth 3:11 and in Prov 31:10 contains more correspondences than the phrase itself. The phrase says something in common on the characterization of Ruth as a person, and of Wisdom personified in Proverbs. They are both capable women who ensure subsistence beyond that of their own. Ruth the *'ēšet hayil* is a Moabite woman seeking survival in the land of Israel. And Lady Wisdom the *'ēšet hayil* is a composite female embodiment who ensures astute subsistence. As an *'ēšet hayil*, Ruth the widow is capable to venture on her dignity for a better future. Personified Wisdom, as an *'ēšet hayil*, is a wife and a mother who is capable of ensuring life-supporting welfare for her household. Yet together they communicate a remarkable feminine role that is strong, competent, and life-giving.

---

[47] Ibid.
[48] Ibid.

PATRIARCHY, A THREAT TO HUMAN BONDING: READING THE STORY OF RUTH IN LIGHT OF MARRIAGE AND FAMILY STRUCTURES IN INDIA

Surekha Nelavala

The book of Ruth has gained much attention from female biblical scholars in general and feminist scholars in particular.[1] The first and

---

[1] While the list is not exhaustive, for diverse feminist readings of the story of Ruth see Athalya Brenner, *The Israelite Woman: Social Role and Literary Type in Biblical Narrative* (Sheffield: Sheffield Academic, 1985), 106–8; Athalya Brenner, "Naomi and Ruth" in *A Feminist Companion to Ruth* (Sheffield: Sheffield Academic, 1993), 70–84; Judith A. Kstes and Gail Twersky Reimer, eds., *Reading Ruth: Contemporary Jewish Women Reclaim a Sacred Story* (New York: Ballantine, 1994), 29–64; Andre LaCocque, "Ruth," *The Feminine Unconventional: Four Subversive Figures in Biblical Tradition* (Minneapolis: Fortress, 1990), 84–116; Amy-Jill Levine, "Ruth," *Women's Bible Commentary*, ed. Carol A. Newsom and Sharon H. Ringe, expanded edition (Louisville: Westminster John Knox, 1998), 84–90; Carol Meyers, ed., *Women in Scripture* (Grand Rapids: Eerdmans, 2000), 252–54; Phyllis Trible "A Human Comedy," *God and the Rhetoric of Sexuality*, ed. K. R. R. Gros Louis and J. S. Ackerman, *Literary Interpretations of Biblical Narratives*, vol. 2 (Nashville: Abingdon, 1982), 161–90; Ilana Pardes, *Countertraditions in the Bible* (Cambridge: Harvard University Press, 1992), 102–3; Kwok Pui-lan, *Postcolonial Imagination and Feminist Theology* (Westminster: John Knox, 2005), 100–122; Madipoane Masenya, "Ruth," *Global Bible Commentary*, ed. Daniel Patte, (Nashville: Abingdon, 2004), 86–91; Renita J. Weems, *Just A Sister Away*, revised and updated (West Bloomfield: Warner, 2005), 27; Julie L. C. Chu, "Returning Home: The Inspiration of the Role Dedifferentiation in the Book of Ruth for Taiwanese Women," *Semeia* 78 (1997): 47–53; Susan Reimer Torn, "Ruth Reconsidered" *Reading Ruth: Contemporary Women Reclaim a Sacred Story*, ed. Judith A. Kates and Gail T. Reimer (New York: Ballantine, 1994), 345–46; Alice Odgen Bells, *Helpmates, Harlots, and Heroes: Women's Stories in the Hebrew Bible* (Louisville: Westminster John Knox, 2007), 183–85; Joan Chittister, *The Story of Ruth: Twelve Moments in Every Woman's Life*, with art by John August Swanson (Grand Rapids: Eerdmans, 2000), 57–78.

foremost attraction is because the book is named after a woman "Ruth," which is in itself uplifting while at the same time providing sufficient scope for feminist interpreters to explore the text to read, interpret, reconstruct, and deconstruct the narration as well as the narrative characters. Some find that the story of Ruth is hopeful and liberating and that the character of Ruth is powerful; others are critical and argue that the book of Ruth is, in fact, reinforcing patriarchal values as Ruth's character simply upholds and submits to patriarchal expectations.

It is interesting to note that when compared to Western feminist scholars, the majority of feminist scholars from different social locations with intersecting perspectives of race, color, or region find the book of Ruth both helpful and liberating, especially when responding to the themes of migration, dislocation, nativity, and otherness that are prominent in the story.[2] My focus in this paper is not to discuss or argue for or against the scholarly research that offers immensely important insight into the reading of the book of Ruth but to discuss Ruth and Naomi's relationship in the light of the household and joint family system. In addition, I will examine the patriarchal dynamics that are common to the ancient household system and the contemporary joint family system in India.

---

[2] Kwok Pui Lan, "Finding a Home for Ruth: Gender, Sexuality, and the Politics of Otherness," *New Paradigms for Bible Study: The Bible in the Third Millennium*, ed. Robert M. Fowler, Edith Blumhofer, and Fernando F. Segovia (New York: T&T Clark, 2004), 141; Madipoane Masenya, "Struggling with Poverty/Emptiness: Rereading the Naomi-Ruth Story in African-South Africa," *Journal of Theology for Southern Africa* 120 (2004): 58; Musa W. Dube, "Divining Ruth for International Relations," in *Other Ways of Reading: African Women and the Bible*, ed. Musa W. Dube (Atlanta: Society of Biblical Literature, 2001), 179–98; Sarojini Nadar, "A South African Indian Womanist Reading of the Character of Ruth," in *Other Ways of Reading: African Women and the Bible*, ed. Musa W. Dube (Atlanta: Society of Biblical Literature, 2001), 171; Chu, "Returning Home," 50–51; Anna May Say Pa, "Reading Ruth 3:1–15 from an Asian Woman's Perspective," in *Engaging the Bible in a Gendered World: An Introduction to Feminist Biblical Interpretation in Honor of Katharine Doob Sakenfeld*, ed. Linda Day and Carolyn Pressler (Louisville: Westminster John Knox, 2006), 47–59; Laura E. Donaldson, "The Sign of Orpah: Reading Ruth through Native Eyes," in *Ruth and Esther, A Feminist Companion to the Bible*, ed. Athalya Brenner, 2nd series (Sheffield: Sheffield Academic Press, 1999), 132.

SISTERHOOD: NAOMI AND RUTH

My reading of the Ruth story deviates insofar as I argue that Ruth and Naomi's choice to cling together is neither a patriarchal attempt nor a feminist move but a choice of a relationship[3] of sisterhood that is established with no terms, expectations, benefits, or rules. Power dynamics do not constitute its premise; instead it is based on understanding a sense of responsibility, accountability, and support.

Ruth and Naomi's bonding is one of mutual empathy in which each gives to the other to the best of her ability. Subsequently, absent from this scene are both patriarchal and feminist dynamics, which have their center in power issues in which the former enforces control of power, while the latter demands an equal share of power. Sisterhood begins with trust, as opposed to feminism or other perspectives which seek rights and justice and begin their hermeneutical principle with suspicion.

This chapter asks why Ruth and Naomi's relationship is typically a difficult one within the parameters of both patriarchy and feminist advocacy. I further examine what must transpire between Ruth and Naomi to create a bond of sisterhood, as well as the dynamics at play in this narration. The lens for my reading comes primarily from knowledge and reflection of the status of a daughter-in-law in her household in the Indian marriage system, where joint family is still prevalent both conceptually and existentially.

THE STORY OF RUTH AND INDIAN MARRIAGE AND FAMILY STRUCTURES

The story of Ruth provides a picture of a typical ancient Israelite household. It bears close similarities with the contemporary joint family system that is both patriarchal and androcentric in nature. Further, it contains elements of domination and oppression, privilege and denial, that are entirely determined by one's gender. Patriarchy and the drive to uphold empirical values are intrinsically hierarchical, which creates a pyramid structure within the family in which power disparities among the individuals ensues. This inherent power imbalance subsequently threatens "family" values in which ideally people are supposed to be bonded in relationships of affection and love. Elements of disruption then enter into family system. However, it is important to mention that most family settings are established with a combination of patriarchal

---

[3] In their introduction, Kstes and Twersky say that the book of Ruth is about women and also about relationship. See Kstes and Twersky, *Reading Ruth: Contemporary Jewish Women Reclaim a Sacred Story*, xviii.

and family values, where, in general, women are socialized to uphold family values, and men are socialized to uphold patriarchal values, and thus contributing to the seemingly smooth administration of a joint family system/household. Having different standards and values for males and females is absolutely justified in patriarchal culture, and it is an accepted norm.

In an ideal setting, the households with an absolute patriarchal system in place turns out to be a happy home, because each one obeys the rules of the patriarch and functions strictly within the established behavioral paradigms. As in the imperial system, where the happiness of the kingdom depends upon the king on the throne, the happiness of the household also depends on the goodness of its patriarch. If a patriarch is naturally a kind-hearted and compassionate person, he carries his power more in terms of responsibility by providing for the needs of the household. However, if the patriarch is a power-centered man, he then leads the household through control via rules and limits as he defines them. While the driving force in the former household is respect, the latter is ruled by fear. Thus some patriarchal households do assure happiness to its members, but it must be kept in mind that the culture, traditions, rules, responsibilities, and expectations are not necessarily established in fairness.

Both in the ancient culture of Israel and in the contemporary culture in India "family" essentially means a household in which the head of the household, his wife, his sons and their wives, and their children live together under the same roof. In such households, patriarchy is the order of the day, and women are regarded as the dependents and men as the providers, even though in Indian culture women are expected to bring a large dowry[4] into her husband's household. In general, in a joint family system in India, as long as the rules are followed and responsibilities carried in absolute obedience, these households often turn out to be happy homes; otherwise there are challenges as the upholders of patriarchy and hierarchy enter into conflict with the challengers of these systems. While it is ideal that all those who enter into this system will commit and subscribe to patriarchy, in practical terms there is always resentment, power struggle, frustrations, and vulnerability with the

---

[4] Dowry is demanded by the groom's family from a bride as an exchange price in marriage, and the dowry asked and given vary depending on the financial status and affordability of a bride, her education, and the economic stability and status of the groom. In most cases, the dowry is a brutal act of demand or price for accepting a bride in marriage, while in few cases it comes as a voluntary gift from a bride's family.

result that less powerful people seek subversive ways to achieve their aims or fulfill their needs.

Patriarchal households and joint family systems appreciate respect, demand sacrifices, and expect obedience. In the context of a culture based upon shame and honor, every major decision is often determined by what brings honor in a given context. Women are not associated with honor; however, they are expected to safeguard themselves and their children from bringing shame or refrain from being shamed. Men are associated with honor and are expected to bring honor to their families through their earnings, popularity, and social status. In the shame and honor dynamic, every decision and action of an individual is judged according to these measures for either approval or rejection, and this depends entirely on the perspective of the patriarch. Consequently, shame and honor are fluid concepts subject to continual change. All members, male and female, young and old, are bound by the customs, traditions, and culture the family has inherited and internalized through active inculcation combined with habit. Again, if the patriarch is a progressive person, there is scope for change or even openness towards thoughtful reconsideration, but if patriarch is conservative and rigid, any change often presents extreme challenges.

The newcomers, primarily the daughters-in-law, are brought into the household with the expectations of extremely rapid adjustments in order to be amicable and integrated into the culture of their new households. The expectations are high: after her wedding, a daughter-in-law must make complete abdication of every aspect of her previous life, as it is often irrelevant how a woman was raised and to what value and behavioral system she was acclimated in the past. The sooner she adjusts, the better for her and for her new household. In other words, a better daughter-in-law is one who is flexible enough to make her new household her own in no time. However, a new daughter-in-law as a stranger and newcomer into the household also faces a certain amount of "otherness," and she is approached with suspicion in addition to the rituals associated with the traditional grand welcome that she may have experienced. Thus, a new daughter-in-law is seen with ambivalence.

RUTH'S FREEDOM OF CHOICE—AN INTERPRETATION

The story of Ruth portrays a household that is somewhat limited in its expansion since only two generations, consisting of six adults, live together: Naomi, Elimelech, two sons Mahlon and Chilion, and the daughters-in-law, Ruth and Orpah. The family quickly loses its structure and becomes a household consisting of three widows, introducing a completely new scenario comprising a nonconforming, all-female household. The three widows, who once belonged to the same household, are no longer related to each other according to kinship definitions per patriarchal understanding. In response to the situation, Naomi suggests to her daughters-in-law that they return to their homes, while declaring to them that she would do the same and return to her home. The scene displays no hard feelings, and there is nothing unusual in Naomi's recommendation. Initially, both Ruth and Orpah react in a similar way to Naomi's suggestion; Orpah kisses Naomi goodbye and yields to Naomi's suggestion, but Ruth insists on remaining with her and thus becomes the heroine of the story.

Although Orpah's depiction is as positive as Ruth's at the outset of the text, Orpah becomes a less desirable daughter-in-law in a patriarchal setting, because she still has strings attaching her to her maternal home. In contrast, Ruth is praised as an ideal figure for shunning her maternal home in order to cling to her mother-in-law in her utmost devotion to her husband's household. The narrator successfully highlights Ruth's character in a patriarchal plot, and she receives due applause for her devotion to her mother-in-law. The fundamental question here is to determine whether her relationship with Naomi has its origin in their mother-in-law and daughter-in-law relationship, or if it derives from their internalized patriarchal boundaries that confined them to Elimelech's household.

The story of Ruth supplies all details after the joint family system was destroyed, leaving no patriarchs/heroes in the household.[5] The women of the household represent a state of utmost vulnerability without the patriarchs. Propagators of any dominant system often rely on this essential vulnerability as their primary argument in favor of "necessary" domination of societal victims. Similarly, the story and the voice of Ruth at a glance is a reminder once again of women's vulnerability and that the lives of women have always been caught within a patriarchal framework.[6] The story of Ruth mirrors the contemporary experiences of a typical daughter-in-law, especially one from the Indian culture, who enters into her husband's household as a complete stranger and an absolute dependent. In patriarchal families, the sons of the house own the household, and the daughters instantly become the loving guests after their respective marriage. Thus, a daughter loses her home without sharing equal privileges with her male siblings, and in her transition to being a wife and daughter-in-law, she is

---

[5] Trible, "A Human Comedy: The Book of Ruth," 162–64.
[6] See e.g., LaCocque, *The Feminine Unconventional*, 170–71.

confronted with the hardest task: to find a home for herself in her husband's household. A daughter-in-law is seen as a stranger and thus a threat to an already existing household, and she enters into marriage under ambivalent conditions.

The first and foremost resistance often comes from a mother-in-law, as well as the unmarried sisters-in-law who are still part of the household due to their unmarried status. The mother is insecure in her transition to being a mother-in-law as there is a threat to share "space" that is equivalent to "power" within the patriarchal framework. Whoever occupies more space around a man in a patriarchal household assumes more power and attention. Thus begins a power game between mother-in-law and daughter-in-law over the space around the man who is held in common between them. Normally, both women turn to subversive means to secure their hold on a man, as each has different roles to play as women in his life. Thus patriarchy, through its central power structure, creates insecurity and unwarranted hostility among the less powerful people within the structure.

Most of the readings agree that the relationship that Ruth and Naomi share is an unusual one, precisely because it is based on sincere love and affection that has clearly moved beyond the polite and cordial relationship, which is often the best that some families can ever hope to achieve.[7] While this is the most common scenario in a patriarchal household, how is it possible for Ruth and Naomi to share a loving relationship? What has liberated them from the patriarchal hostility that normally exists between a mother-in-law and daughter-in-law? Ruth commits herself to an old woman in a world where life depends upon men; there is no hope of material or personal gain, and she has chosen a position of responsibility and solidarity.[8]

In the book of Ruth, Naomi wants to go back to her family and people once her husband has died. She finds that her native land is better off, as the Lord has brought prosperity to it. Perhaps Naomi has been building an argument to return home, and she justifies her decision by pointing to the Lord's intervention on behalf of her people. Similarly, Orpah, the other daughter-in-law, returns to her own home town and people, as her husband has died and thus there is no household for her anymore. However, Ruth—unlike the typical daughter-in-law— expresses her wish to go with Naomi, rather than go back to her people. Ruth does not cling to Naomi for her own benefit, but in solidarity with

---

[7] Ilana Pardes, *Countertraditions in the Bible*, 103.
[8] Yair Zakovitch, *Ruth: Introduction and Commentary*, Mikra le-Yisrael (Tel Aviv: Am Oved, 1990), 61.

an aged widow, as her words indicate: "Do not press me to desert you, to resist following you; for wherever you go, I too will go; whatever your shelter, I will share it; your people will become mine, and your Divine Being will be my own. Wherever you die, I will die, and be buried alongside. May Yahweh strike me at any time with afflictions, if anything but death parts us" (Ruth 1:16–17). In other words, Ruth urges Naomi to understand that she is disheartened to let go of the aged widow.

Ruth acts much differently from the ideal daughter-in-law, who has a connection to her husband's household only through her man and nothing else. There is no scope and opportunity for two women to forge a connection or relationship through their own independent action in a patriarchal household. After a man dies, ideally the woman has no continued connection unless she enters into a Levirate marriage. Thus Ruth and Naomi's bonding is not within the boundaries of Elimelech's household but outside of that household. Ruth's actions reflect her new freedom and her choice to forge a new relationship with Naomi.

Ruth: A Liberationist and Humanist

To explain my reading in further detail: Orpah demonstrates obedience to and respect for Naomi by returning to her own family, as she does not want to become a burden on her widowed mother-in-law. However, when Ruth is asked to go back to her people, she resists and expresses instead her determination to follow Naomi until death separates them (Ruth 1:16–17). In so doing, Ruth is not fulfilling the role of a good daughter-in-law; rather she transcends the daughter-in-law role and establishes a new relationship between the two women, not one based on the hierarchal power structure that would have existed within their former patriarchal/kyriarchal household (presumably under Elimelech) but one of equality, a woman-to-woman relationship of sisterhood that gave both of them the liberty to act differently from their expected social roles. Because of the deaths of their husbands, Naomi, Orpah and Ruth have been freed from the rules, expectations, and boundaries of a patriarchal household. This allows Ruth to stand by Naomi out of freedom, not out of desperation or compulsion that resulted from vulnerability, loneliness, and powerlessness. Thus the relationship that these women share with each other is not of a mother-in-law and daughter-in-law, where hierarchal power is the central focus, but that of a woman-to-woman—of mother-to-daughter or even true sisterhood—

where the focus is on empathy, care, and support for one another. They share a new relationship that is free from patriarchal enforcement.[9]

In short, given my Indian context and understanding of the mother and daughter-in law relationship in a joint family system—which is typically a cordial one at best, not a true, heartfelt one—I see Ruth's insistence on joining Naomi as a reflection of a deep, meaningful relationship that has developed between them. The natural thing would have been for Ruth to follow Orpah's course of action and go back to her family and her people. There, perhaps, she would have resumed her subservient role in her father's household. Like other readers of the book, I admire Ruth for staying with Naomi, but I do so for different reasons. Ruth is a liberationist and a humanist in my opinion who acts outsides of traditional influences and according to what she thought is just and right while exercising her freedom in responsibility.

---

[9] See Pardes, *Countertraditions in the Bible*, 102–3.

THE BOAZ SOLUTION: READING RUTH IN LIGHT OF AUSTRALIAN ASYLUM SEEKER DISCOURSE

Anthony Rees

PREAMBLE—INITIAL PROBLEMS

It may appear unusual for a contribution from a white Australian man to appear in a volume that locates itself in Asia. Perhaps not. This dichotomy reflects something of my country's lack of belonging, its identity crisis. To whom do we belong? Why? How? Or is it enough to just be Australian? If we are part of Asia, we are certainly on the margins, geographically. But the push towards Asia suggests a desire to be more central, a recognition that being isolated is a disadvantage. Political maneuvering towards Asia seems to be a way of overcoming our distance from the center, our dissatisfaction with marginalization, and our anxiety with our identity.

But this creates a further problem: what is Asia? Asia is a hugely diverse space, incorporating a richness of people, culture, and language far beyond our experience. It is in some sense reductionist and essentialist to talk of Asia, as Edward Said has warned us.[1] What draws Manila and Mumbai together? Doha and Dhaka? Colombo and Kyoto? Or to push a little further, Hobart and Ho Chi Minh, Perth and Peshawar, Canberra and Kabul? To understand Asia in a singular fashion is to make the same mistake that is commonly made about the world's most invisible region, our natural neighbors, the Pacific.

And how does Australia share this imaginary Asian experience? Who do we imagine when we talk of "Asians"? Is it the lady who writes my prescriptions or the girl that is offered to me as I walk the streets in Asian cities? Is it the young man in the fancy suit and car carving out a career in the court house or the boy making my shirts in Bangladesh? Are the doctor and the lawyer Asian? Or Australian? Identity issues again surface.

---

[1] Edward W. Said, *Orientalism* (London: Penguin, 2003).

None of this is to make an argument for or against Australia's position in Asia. But rather, it establishes that Asia's boundaries are fluid, both in terms of geography and identity. This fluidity invites this discussion of Australia's place, or belonging, in Asia.

It is true to say that Asia has a strong presence in Australia. There are suburbs in Sydney where shop signs are written in Chinese, and where a person who speaks English is hard to find. Migration, both forced and voluntary, has altered the shape of our communities and, indeed, continues to do so. As this Asian presence has increased in Australia, perhaps it has been a natural thing for us to explore our relationship with Asia, to perhaps even become "Asian" in some sense. There is a "migration" taking place away from our Pacific family to the bigger, brighter opportunities offered by Asia. This is not a forced migration, but rather a migration of force, of expediency.

Having highlighted problems of identity but offering few solutions, I have prepared the way for my offering which follows. It picks up these very themes, engaging Australia's own recent policies regarding those who have sought refuge in Australia. It then turns to the story of Ruth, where these issues also emerge. I hope that it does not do what I fear Australia's Asian turn does: assume superiority.

More Problems, and Attempted Solutions

In September 2001, the Australian Parliament passed into law a piece of legislation commonly referred to as the "Pacific Solution." The Pacific Solution emerged from a particular problem: the arrival in Australian waters of boats carrying asylum seekers. In simple terms, boats departing from Indonesia that were intercepted by Australian Navy vessels would be redirected to third countries, where they were held while their applications for asylum were processed. These centers were in Nauru, Christmas Island,[2] and Papua New Guinea's Manus Island.[3] The legislation passed with the support of both of the major parties. The bill came quickly after the "Tampa Affair," in which a Norwegian ship

---

[2] Christmas Island differs slightly from the others in this list, insofar as it is a non-self-governing territory of Australia.

[3] Discussions also took place with Kiribati, Tonga, Tuvalu, Palau, East Timor, and France (in relation to the possible use of French Polynesia). See Janet Phillips, "The 'Pacific Solution' Revisited: A Statistical Guide to the Asylum Seeker Caseloads on Nauru and Manus Island," Parliament of Australia, http://www.aph.gov.au/About_Parliament/Parliamentary_Departments/Parliamentary_Library/pubs/BN/2012-2013/PacificSolution.

that had come to the aid of a distress signal was denied access to Australian waters, despite carrying over four hundred asylum seekers, some suffering acute medical conditions. The ship's captain eventually disregarded the instruction and entered Australian territorial waters.[4] Australian soldiers intercepted the vessel and ordered the Captain to return to international waters, a request denied by the captain. Eventually, the asylum seekers, found by medical staff to be dehydrated and suffering from a range of medical ailments, were loaded onto an Australian Naval vessel and transported to Nauru. Just weeks later, the "children overboard" scandal took place. The issue of asylum seeking was front-and-center in Australia's public life.

The Pacific Solution became a case of good timing for the John Howard led conservative government. The border control issue and the government's strong stance gained popular support. Launching the 2001 election campaign, Howard declared, "We will decide who comes to this country and the circumstances in which they come."[5] The line was repeated in television advertisements in the lead up to the poll, and the conservative government won the election with an increased majority. The Pacific Solution was intended to be a deterrent to those seeking asylum, the assumption being that if it was perceived by asylum seekers that one would not reach Australia but instead be ferried off to another location, then Australia would no longer be such an attractive target.

Without question, there was a slowing of arrivals in Australian waters in the subsequent years. However, this is not necessarily to be attributed to the policy of the Howard government. This was a period of decreased migration and, notably, the time in which the Taliban regime of Afghanistan, one of the primary sources of refugees, was overthrown.

In late 2007, Kevin Rudd led the Australian Labor Party to power. In the years since the implementation of the Pacific Solution, increased anxiety about the state of the facilities and the psychological impact of detention experience on the refugees had created a certain discomfort with the arrangements. Refugee advocates agitated for change, pointing to the lack of sanitation, water, and electricity for the harshly housed

---

[4] The ship's captain, Arne Rinnan, demonized by the Australian government, was later awarded Norway's highest civic honor. The crew of his ship were awarded the Nansen Refugee award by UNHCR for their efforts to follow internationally agreed principles for aiding people in distress at sea.
[5] Sarah Clarke, "Liberals Accused of Trying to Rewrite History," Australian Broadcasting Corporation, http://www.abc.net.au/lateline/content/2001/s422692.htm.

detainees.⁶ A 2007 report outlined the mental health issues confronted by, in particular, women and children and highlighted the instances of food strike and other forms of self-harm.⁷ By February 2008, the Pacific Solution was cut adrift by the new Government, to the praise of the United Nations High Commission for Refugees. New immigration minister, Chris Evans described the Pacific Solution as a "cynical, costly and ultimately unsuccessful exercise."⁸

Within a few years, boat arrivals into Australian waters had again become a significant political issue. Pressure mounted, but Prime Minister Rudd declared that he would not "lurch to the right" on the asylum seeker issue, a move which proved costly to him.⁹ Deputy leader, Julia Gillard, with the support of factional leaders moved on Rudd, displacing him as Prime Minister. Initially, Gillard's team continued the policies of Rudd, but under the increasing pressure of boat arrivals, a new idea was born: the ill-fated "Malaysia Solution."

The Malaysia solution was intended to be a "swap" between Australia and Malaysia. Eight hundred people who had attempted to reach Australia by boat would be deported to Malaysia. In return, Australia would accept four thousand people from Malaysia who had been found to be genuine refugees over a four year period.¹⁰ The plan attracted the ire of refugee advocates, and the legislation was challenged and declared unlawful in the High Court. Despite attempts to make necessary amendments to the bill, the opposition parties refused to support the changes, and the Malaysian Solution was dead in the water.¹¹

Opposition leader Tony Abbott was by this stage gaining great popular support through his three-word sloganeering, most commonly

---

⁶ Phillips, "'Pacific Solution' Revisited."
⁷ Ibid.
⁸ AAP. "Flight from Nauru Ends Pacific Solution," *Sydney Morning Herald*, 8 February 2008, http://news.smh.com.au/national/flight-from-nauru-ends-pacific-solution-20080208-1qww.html.
⁹ Phillip Coorey, "Gillard on the Front Foot, Lurches to Right, But Team Rudd Not Beaten," *Sydney Morning Herald*, 20 August 2012, http://www.smh.com.au/federal-politics/political-opinion/gillard-on-the-front-foot-lurches-to-right-but-team-rudd-not-beaten-20120819-24gf0.html.
¹⁰ AAP, "Gillard Announces Malaysian Solution," *Sydney Morning Herald*, 7 May 2011, www.smh.com.au/national/gillard-announces-malaysian-solution-20110507-1ed0h.html.
¹¹ Ting Walker, "The High Court Decision on the Malaysian Solution," Australian Capital Territory, 25 November, 2011, http://www.abc.net.au/local/stories/2011/11/23/3374312.htm.

declaring his capacity to "stop the boats." With pressure continuing to mount on the Gillard government and calls coming from all quarters for the reinstitution of the Pacific Solution, centers on Nauru and Manus Island reopened in August 2012. However, as Gillard's popularity continued to wane and the opposition's "stop the boats" mantra intensified, Kevin Rudd returned to the Prime Minister's office in June 2013, with the hope that his popular appeal could turn the fortunes of the Labor Party ahead of the impending election.

Despite his earlier comment, that he would never lurch to the right on asylum seeker policy, less than a month after returning to office, Rudd signed an agreement with the Prime Minister of Papua New Guinea, Peter O'Neill. Under the agreement, Rudd declared

> From now on, any asylum seeker who arrives in Australia by boat will have no chance of being settled in Australia as refugees. Asylum seekers taken to Christmas Island will be sent to Manus and elsewhere in Papua New Guinea for assessment of their refugee status. If they are found to be genuine refugees they will be resettled in Papua New Guinea.... If they are found not to be genuine refugees they may be repatriated to their country of origin or be sent to a safe third country other than Australia. These arrangements are contained within the Regional Resettlement Arrangement signed by myself and the Prime Minister of Papua New Guinea just now.[12]

It was widely agreed that the "Regional Resettlement Plan" signed with Papua New Guinea was an even more harsh arrangement than the Pacific Solution and was no more than a cynical political move.[13] The opposition, with their hardline "stop the boats" rhetoric could hardly raise an objection and so this gave the struggling government some breathing space. But the heavy lurch to the right also served to anger the Greens, refugee advocates, human rights groups, and the element of Australian society that was already angered by the cruelty of the off-shore detention processes.

During the final years of this tumultuous time, the dehumanization of asylum seekers and the coarse political rhetoric about them was widely noted. Current immigration minister Scott Morrison has

---

[12] "Pacific Solution," Wikipedia, http://en.wikipedia.org/wiki/Pacific_Solution.
[13] Dennis Shanahan, "PM Lurches in Bid to Right Labor's Ship," *The Australian*, 20 July 2013, http://www.theaustralian.com.au/opinion/columnists/pm-lurches-in-bid-to-right-labors-ship/story-e6frg75f-1226682255779#.

defended his department's use of the term "illegal arrival"[14] to describe those arriving by boat. National broadcaster, the ABC, countered by refusing to allow their journalists to use the expression. Morrison reiterated that he was aware that seeking asylum was not illegal and that his term referenced mode of arrival. Of course, the logic of this is faulty. One seeks asylum in the way that they can. Singling out those who arrive on boats is simply playing a political game. Further, people lamented the reality that the reduction of humans to labels or categories was a political attempt to suppress the natural emotion this issue carries: "illegal arrivals," "boat people," and "asylum seekers" are categories that in some way attempt to mask the humanity of those seeking refuge. In doing so, it is forgotten that these people, mothers and fathers, brothers and sisters, young and old, are all in situations of great vulnerability. It is forgotten that many of them have left in traumatic circumstances, leaving loved ones behind in the hope of grasping hold of life while there is still a chance. Instead, their actions are incorrectly labeled illegal, and their humanity reduced to a "problem."

What has not been addressed adequately is the nomenclature of this suite of legislative instruments created to address the situation. The persistent use of the term "solution" implies the recognition of a "problem," and also serves as a dehumanizing element. Perhaps worse, it leaves the "problem," the actual humans involved, out of the descriptor. Instead, the recipient of the problem is placed at the center. This is an unfortunate circumstance, especially given that those who take on Australia's "problem" are nations that lack the immense financial and natural resources of Australia. One of the great ironies of the arrangement with Papua New Guinea was Prime Minister O'Neill's comment that Papua New Guinea had a lot of uninhabited regions and so had plenty of space to accommodate the refugees!

Nonetheless, this notion of problem-solution in regards to humans is not a new one, particularly in regards to migration. I propose a reading of Ruth that engages this unfortunate terminology. While the application of the Australian situation to the narrative is far from precise, as will be seen, it is still instructive and creates a new way of understanding the actions of Naomi as well as the dynamics of power in the real life situation confronting asylum seekers in Australia.

---

[14] Emma Griffiths, "Immigration Minister Scott Morrison Defends Use of Term 'Illegal Arrivals,' Plays Down PNG Police Incident," http://www.abc.net.au/news/2013-10-21/immigration-minister-scott-morrison-defends-use-of-illegals-term/5035552.

A Problem Called Ruth

The book of Ruth begins with a story of refugees. A man, Elimelech, takes his wife and two sons from their home in Judah to the country of Moab on account of a famine that had beset their homeland. The narrator places the story "in the days when the judges ruled" (Ruth 1:1), which, readers of the bible know, were times of great instability in the political sphere.[15] Given the literary interplay, it is no surprise that famine in a time of civic unrest may be a factor in a family seeking refuge elsewhere.

However, as is often the case, the immigration of Elimelech and his family is not a smooth one. Rather than happily settling in their new home, Elimelech dies, leaving Naomi a widow and his sons without a father. Soon, it seems, both sons marry Moabite women. One can hardly be surprised at this. We might imagine that Naomi is happy for her sons to have found wives and be able to forge lives for themselves, a pride and hope common to parents everywhere. However, the family is overwhelmed by tragedy.[16] In the space of ten years, Naomi is left without husband and without child, a fate shared by her two Moabite daughters-in-law.

Driven again by both desperation and opportunity, Naomi seeks to return home, having heard of the Lord's provision for the people of Judah (Ruth 1:6). She sets out with her daughters-in-law but at some point in the journey urges them to return home. This is an unusual event. There is no indication of any discussion prior to this, just an indication that the three widows are travelling together. The NRSV highlights this sudden change by translating the *waw*-consecutive as "but," although there is no compelling grammatical reason for this choice. Bush notes that Naomi "frontally attack[s] the problem,"[17] while Holmstedt mentions the "economy of the narrative."[18] Bush simply translates the verb in the past tense, while Holmstedt uses the sequential "then." In any case, the introduction of the conversation between the three women comes as a shock, particularly given Naomi's timing. Holmstedt rightly points out that this parting was the sensible option. The widowed young

---

[15] This is not to argue this date for the provenance of the work. Scholars are generally agreed that the text lies somewhere in the late-exilic to postexilic period. Eunny Lee, "Ruth, Book of," in *The New Interpreter's Dictionary of the Bible*, ed. K. D. Sakenfeld, vol. 4. (Nashville: Abingdon, 2009), 867 (865–68).
[16] Lee, "Ruth," 865.
[17] Frederic William Bush, *Ruth, Esther* (Waco, TX: Word Books, 1996), 85.
[18] Robert D. Holmstedt, *Ruth: A Handbook on the Hebrew Text* (Waco, TX: Baylor University Press, 2010), 71.

women stand a better chance at finding husbands in their own land and can find provision amongst their own kin,[19] which Ruth points out. "Turn back," she urges them. She reminds them of her inability to provide husbands for them, her inability to provide any meaningful provision.[20] Why bring the women this far and then implore them to leave, with the emotional drain of tearing away from home already done?

Trible highlights two things which are relevant to our discussion. Firstly, Naomi has been stripped of all identity. Without husband and child, she is alone. So too, her daughters-in-law. Secondly, despite their "oneness," there is still a power dynamic at play: Age commands youth.[21] Orpah eventually bends to Naomi's will and does what is "sane and reasonable ... sound, sensible and secure."[22] Ruth however, chooses to resist and consciously determines to abandon her national identity, her religious identity, and the possibility of a future husband and family. Indeed, there is a sense in which having come this far, she has already left these things behind, already broken away from humanly constructed realities. A return may well be impossible for Ruth.[23]

Ruth's language is ambiguous. Holmstedt translates Ruth 1:16 "Do not press me to abandon you, to turn from going after you."[24] The word "abandon" is an interesting one. It is Naomi who is departing, the one who is leaving things behind. Naomi paints Ruth's possible journey with her as a type of abandonment: Ruth would be leaving the possibility of a good future behind were she to continue with her. And there appears to have been no attempt made by Ruth and Orpah to dissuade Naomi from taking this journey, so it seems they were confident in her ability to last the distance. Certainly, there appears to be a sincerity in the daughters-in law's affection to Naomi, demonstrated in Ruth 1:14. But they are under no obligation to her. So why then does Ruth speak of abandoning Naomi? Why is she so determined to follow? Why, in the face of Naomi's

---

[19] Ibid, 72.
[20] Ilona Rashkow, "Ruth: The Discourse of Power and the Power of Discourse," in *A Feminist Companion to Ruth*, ed. Athalya Brenner (Shefield: Sheffield Phoenix, 1993), 30 (26–41).
[21] Phyllis Trible, *God and the Rhetoric of Sexuality* (Philadelphia: Fortress, 1978), 169.
[22] Ibid, 172.
[23] Rashkow, "Ruth," 32.
[24] Holmstedt, *Ruth*, 67.

almost over-powering authority, does she have the courage to issue a command of her own: "Do not press me to abandon you"?[25]

As Elizabeth Cady Stanton noted, Naomi has a "peculiar magnetic attraction" for Ruth.[26] To use the contemporary language of migration, Naomi seems to represent a "pull factor." Against Naomi's insistence that Ruth returns, Ruth counters that where Naomi goes, she too will go. Is this determination due to her sense of allegiance to Naomi? Or might Naomi represent some other thing? Is it Naomi whom Ruth fears abandoning or something else?

We know already that Naomi's return is motivated by a report that the land of Judah is flourishing again, so much so, that it compels Naomi to undertake a journey home. This might suggest to us that food is not so easy to come by in Moab, that survival was difficult. We must assume that Ruth also is aware of this change in circumstances in Judah, and likewise, as a widow, we must assume that life was difficult also for her. After all, it appears that she was willing to leave her past behind to travel with Naomi. So perhaps we might imagine that Ruth is dreaming of something else: a better place, a brighter future, a fresh beginning. So it is possible that when Ruth speaks of abandoning Naomi, she is actually more concerned with abandoning a future she has dreamt for herself. The person of Naomi represents Ruth's opportunity to escape the tragedy and difficulty of her own life: a childless widow in a difficult land. Push and pull factors come together. Ruth understands the truths of Naomi's reasoning but imagines another outcome.

It is possible that Naomi was aware of this possibility, and it could well be that this lies behind her efforts to dissuade Ruth and Orpah. She understands that Ruth and Orpah represent a burden to her that she would rather do without,[27] insofar as they are outsiders to the Bethlehem community. That is to say, they are a problem for her, and convincing them to stay behind is a legitimate solution. But she did not count on Ruth's stubborn resilience.

Ruth's determination to create a new future for herself is witnessed in her initiative and industry.[28] Not waiting for Naomi's guidance, she resolves to go and work in the fields, both a method of provision but also assimilation into society. Brenner notes that the language of "love" that Naomi uses in Ruth 1:16–17 implies a legal contract. That is, Ruth is

---

[25] Rashkow, "Ruth," 30.
[26] Elizabeth C. Stanton, "The Book of Ruth," in *A Feminist Companion to Ruth,* ed. Athalya Brenner (Sheffield: Sheffield Academic Press, 1993), 21 (20–25).
[27] Tod Linafelt, *Ruth* (Collegeville: Liturgical Press, 1999), 15.
[28] Stanton, "The Book of Ruth," 22

committing to take care of Naomi,[29] though this contractual agreement does not appear to find an expression in the story. We see no pressure from Naomi for Ruth to go out and care for her. Indeed, as we will see, it seems that even as Ruth goes out to work, Naomi persists in pondering a possible solution.[30] Ruth seems aware of her legal right as a foreigner to engage in this behavior, and so she goes to the field to glean.[31] Unwittingly ("as it happened," Ruth 2:3) she finds herself in the field of Naomi's relative, who is unaware of her presence in his field or of her identity (Ruth 2:5). Ruth has impressed all with her determination.[32] It makes her visible, even while highlighting the desperation and poverty of her circumstances.[33] When approached by Boaz, she throws herself before him, her language again highlighting her vulnerability. Boaz, like Naomi, positions himself as the powerful figure but, unlike Naomi, displays his capacity to protect and provide for her.

A Solution Emerges, But for Whom?

Returning home that evening to Naomi, Ruth speaks of Boaz, and Naomi reveals the nature of their kinship (Ruth 2:20). Seeing an unexpected opportunity and one that has only arisen on account of Ruth's industry, Naomi endorses the things Boaz has said and urges her to stay close to the young women in the field so as not to be "bothered." Then, after an unspecified amount of time, Naomi engages the "Boaz Solution."

At the beginning of chapter 3, Naomi instructs Ruth to go and approach Boaz. This is done in order to seek security for her. To be clear, Naomi is sending a vulnerable, foreign woman, washed, anointed, and well-dressed to a place I imagine to be full of drinking men. This hardly seems to be a strategy concerned with Ruth's security. Naomi is aware that Boaz represents a major opportunity, not only for Ruth, but for herself also. Indeed, even more so for Naomi. She can have her field

---

[29] Athalya Brenner, "Ruth as Foreign Worker and the Politics of Exogamy," in *Ruth and Esther*, ed. A. Brenner (Sheffield: Sheffield Academic, 1999), 159 (158–62).

[30] Imtraud Fischer, "The Book of Ruth: A 'Feminist' Commentary to the Torah?" in *Ruth and Esther*, ed. A. Brenner (Sheffield: Sheffield Academic, 1999), 29 (24–49).

[31] Ibid, 28.

[32] Rashkow, "Ruth," 34.

[33] As Brenner notes, foreign workers are invisible to the dominant culture, and the only way to become visible is by trying harder, by exceeding the efforts of the local workers (Brenner, "Ruth as Foreign Worker," 160).

redeemed and move Ruth on, gaining security for herself and ridding herself of a burden. It is not only the field which could be redeemed, but Naomi as well.[34]

In short, Ruth becomes someone else's problem. Ruth plays her role beautifully, surpassing what Naomi had asked of her. Her charged, seductive language to Boaz again highlights her vulnerability, and Boaz, perhaps flattered by the attentions of the young foreign lady, commits to assist, sending her home with a very generous amount of supply and promising to resolve the matters urgently. Boaz expresses his admiration at Ruth's devotion (3:10). Brenner notes that such devotion, like hard work, is a way by which the foreigner can become noticed but that it is only by marriage that full assimilation can be achieved.[35] Ruth, the problem, becomes objectified. She becomes the object of Naomi's plan and of Boaz's desire. Naomi's plan is continuing in a fashion she could scarcely have imagined.

The great success of the Boaz solution is evidenced in the great boon that it is for Naomi. The marriage of Ruth and Boaz is blessed by the city elders and results in the birth of a boy. The women celebrate the restoration of Naomi's line through the boy, and Naomi takes the child to her own breast and nurses him. The women continue to sing: "A child is born to Naomi!" What's more, the boy, Obed, becomes the grandfather of Israel's greatest King, David. Perhaps not surprisingly, the problem, Ruth, and the solution, Boaz, disappear. They lose subjectivity.[36] Indeed, as Brenner suggests elsewhere, throughout this whole story, Ruth may have had far less choice than we fondly remember.[37] Naomi, in some sense the architect of the whole story, retains hers and emerges as the real beneficiary of the solution.

An Ending

As was mentioned previously, it is not reasonable to expect to see a "like-for-like" relationship between these two texts: the text of Ruth and the text of contemporary immigration discourse. And yet read together, the subtle playing of power is highlighted in both. Ultimately, it is the

---

[34] Athalya Brenner, "Naomi and Ruth," in *A Feminist Companion to Ruth*, ed. Athalya Brenner (Sheffield: Sheffield Academic, 1993), 71 (70–84).
[35] Brenner, "Ruth as Foreign Worker," 160.
[36] Athalya Brenner, "Naomi and Ruth: Further Reflections," in *A Feminist Companion to Ruth*, ed. Athalya Brenner (Sheffield: Sheffield Academic, 1993), 141 (140–44).
[37] Brenner, "Ruth as Foreign Worker," 159.

one who designs the solution that stands to gain most. Australian governments have been quick to talk up the great benefits to the host countries that have been engaged through the various solutions concocted. But are those gains substantial enough, given that they are a pay-off for dealing with Australia's problem? In Ruth, Boaz is the solution. What does he gain for taking on Naomi's problem? The son born to him appears to become Naomi's child. And as he explains to the other kinsman in Ruth 4:5–6, marrying Ruth brings with it a host of other responsibilities, which are beyond the willingness of the rightful redeemer. The latter was unwilling to be the solution, for the cost was too great.

The invisibility of the migrant has also been highlighted. Invisibility acts as a synonym here for powerlessness. Ruth is invisible on her arrival in Bethlehem and has to struggle to find favor. Even then, she is the object of others, obeying the commands of her mother-in-law, and making herself vulnerable to a stranger she hopes might be able to help her. Ruth's speech also points to this: "I am a foreigner" (Ruth 2:10); "May I continue to find favor in your sight" (Ruth 2:13); "All that you tell me to do I will do" (Ruth 3:5); "I am Ruth, your handmaid" (Ruth 3:9). Even at the moment of her acceptance into her new culture, she disappears, and the powerful figure continues to dominate the story. This invisibility is seen in the contemporary debates around asylum seekers by the reduction of humanity to categories: boat-people, illegal entries and so on. The asylum seeker, the refugee, instead of being seen as a person, a subject, becomes an object, a problem. Abstracted, they become invisible. Ironically, it is their humanity that is the real problem. The solution has been dehumanization, or in other words, suppression of the problem. It is a real problem. We are a long way from a solution.

STIRRING NAOMI: ANOTHER GLEANING AT THE EDGES OF RUTH 1

Jione Havea

Naomi is one of the characters in the complex and unsettling story that biblical and interpretive traditions consign for Ruth; Naomi is the woman in another woman's gig. To bring Naomi out of Ruth's shadows, i[1] propose a reading that is openly transgressive.[2] I want Naomi to have her own story, agenda and plot, which at places deviate from those of Ruth.

That Naomi manages the plot from Ruth 1:6 onward is relatively easy to see. Naomi gets up to return, and she begins to have a say in who goes and what happens in the story-world. But Naomi was controlling the plot even before Ruth 1:6. Naomi was driving things from the very beginning. Before Ruth was conceived in the narrator's account, Naomi was already igniting the plot. And so i glean for Naomi in the fields of Ruth's story.[3]

Naomi's story starts in emptiness and in motion and has many twists and turns, before ending back at the place where it began. Naomi crossed cultural, linguistic, and ideological borders when she, with her

---

[1] I use lowercase "i," because i use the lowercase with "you," "she," "they," and "others." I do not see the point in capitalizing the first person when s/he *is* in relation to everyone/everything else.

[2] Thinking that all readings are transgressive, in that they interfere with, and cross into, the text(s) in order to determine their meanings, i claim that my reading is "openly transgressive," because i am aware of my transgressions. And realizing that i might miss the points of the text, i confess that my reading is transgressive at another level.

[3] Jennifer L. Koosed, *Gleaning Ruth: A Biblical Heroine and Her Afterlives* (Columbia: The University of South Carolina Press, 2011), 6: "To glean is to follow behind, picking up what others leave. Gleaning was, and is, a common agricultural activity but most of us no longer live in communities that are familiar with it. Contemporary gleaning in industrialized and urbanized cultures consists of a wide range of other practices. The context has changed, but the impulse to pick through, to pick up, and assemble anew has hardly abated."

husband and two sons, departed Bethlehem of Judah in search of refuge in the fields of Moab (Ruth 1:1). A famine had fallen on their hometown, whose name ironically means "house of food/bread" (בת־לחם). The stockroom of Judah was empty, so Naomi and her family uprooted and abandoned their relatives and friends and, with a hint of satire, they looked for life in a land and among a people that Judeans considered God-forsaken.[4] They were pushed out of their home, and so, to use an image from my island setting, they jumped off the boat into a sea of fire (allusion to the Pacific volcanic Rim of Fire).

Famine, abandonment, migration. Naomi and her family joined a long line of people who opt to drift (migrate, seeking refuge) because of some form of famine. This line extends back to Abram and Sarai (Gen 12:10),[5] who departed not too long (in narrative time) after they arrived in Canaan, the land that Yhwh promised for them and their descendants, a land that was occupied upon their arrival (Gen 12:6b). Yhwh gave occupied land and a fruitless promise. Famine strikes regularly in the biblical account, and one might argue that such conditions were expected after Yhwh cursed the ground in the garden narrative (Gen 3:17–19). Thanks to Yhwh's curse, famines became part of living. In response to famines some people move to fertile lands for refuge (like Egypt and Moab), but some stay behind in their famine stricken homes. Surviving famines formed the human and vulnerable creatures, who may flee if they choose, whereas earth had to find ways to endure and renew itself.

I imagine that migration in the biblical world, as in contemporary settings, was an option available to the privileged members of the society. They would be aware of the world outside their borders, know something about foreign languages and cultures, and they could afford to relocate and to reestablish themselves in new lands.[6] Interestingly, when they return after the famine, they find that those who did not

---

[4] Danna N. Fewell and David M. Gunn, *Compromising Redemption: Relating Characters in the Book of Ruth* (Louisville: Westminster John Knox, 1990), 25. See Koosed, *Gleaning Ruth*, 29–34.

[5] Forced migration occurred in the stories leading up to the appearance of Abram. Cain was marked and forced out of his home (Gen 4), and so were the peoples who drowned in the story of Noah (Gen 6–9) and dispersed in the story of Babel (Gen 11). For an alternative reading of Cain's story, see my "To Love Cain More Than God, in Other Words, 'Nody' Gen 4:1–16," in *Levinas and Biblical Studies*, ed. Tamara C. Eskenazi, Gary A. Phillips, and David Jobling (Atlanta: Society of Biblical Literature, 2003), 91–112.

[6] While all asylum seekers leave their home and native land, only those with wealth can pay smugglers to take them across borders and the seas.

move (the un- and underprivileged) survived the wrath of the famine. The remnant that survived the famine exhibit the endurance and wisdom that one finds among the "people of the land" (read: indigenous people) who know how to survive in desperate situations. Given the signifying name of Naomi's husband, 'Elimelech ("my God [is] king" or "my God kings;" אלי־מלך), an owner of property and inheritance in Judah (cf. Ruth 4:3–6), i suspect that Naomi's family was a privileged one. Was she a privileged woman in her own right (apart from her husband)? In a patriarchal world where there is not much that suggests privileges for a woman as bearing a son does, it is revealing to note that Naomi, like Eve, Rebekkah and Asenath, had two sons. She was not an empty woman when the family departed for Moab. She "went away full" (Ruth 1:21). Naomi was full, but her story puts her in an empty and transitory world.

Did Naomi go willingly to Moab? Did Elimelech consult her about the move or was she taken, dragged along, to Moab? If Naomi was a Tongan mother, i would argue that she had a say in her family's migration. Tongan mothers are more concerned than Tongan fathers tend to be about putting food in front of their children. Like other Polynesian islands, Tonga is very patriarchal, and men do most of the gardening (on plots of land outside of the homes) and fishing while women are in charge of the home and with sustaining the family. In times of hardship, men are too stubborn to ask for help or to move,[7] which would reveal that they failed to provide. Mothers, on the other hand, would move for the sake of their children. Even (or, especially) in a patriarchal setting, mothers are expected to provide and sustain. As someone who comes from a similar background, i imagine that Naomi had masterminded her family's migration to Moab. The narrative suggests this possibility, for she decided to move back to Judah later when she heard that food was available there again (Ruth 1:6). She exhibited agency in coming to (note her explanation "i went away full" instead of "we went away full" in Ruth 1:21) and leaving Moab, moving to where she could find resources. Naomi appears to have been driven by a determination to survive. *'Oku taki holo ia 'e hono kete* (Tongan saying: "s/he is led around by her/his stomach"). The question for me then is not whether Elimelech consulted Naomi about moving to Moab, but whether Elimelech had any say in the move at all. In this regard, there is no reason for Naomi to be naïve or passive in Ruth 1:1–2. Her story opens with lack and motion, but she was firm and rooted.

---

[7] Some fathers (e.g., Lot in Gen 19) and husbands (e.g., a Levite in Judges 19) do move, but usually as a last resort and for the sake of their reputations.

There is no reason also for Naomi to loath Moab or its people.[8] Moab is a problem for Abrahamic traditionalists and for pro-Israelite biblicists (cf. Gen 19:30–38), but Naomi does not come across as such a one. The narrator is no Abrahamic traditionalist either. He turns the page on Israel's history with this narrative, starting a new chapter that looks ahead to David as the forthcoming main character (Ruth 4:17). That very David looked back to Moab when he needed to find refuge for his parents (1 Sam 22:3). The narrator remembers something about Jacob through Rachel and Leah (Ruth 4:11) and something about Judah through Tamar (Ruth 4:12), but Abraham has passed, and Moses is not in his script. Naomi thus migrated with her family during a shift in the memory of Israel's narrative. David is rising over the horizon. Naomi is on the move, rousing all the way to Moab and then back.

When her husband drops dead (with no explanation given) in Ruth 1:3, Naomi is left in charge of the family and the continuation of the narrative.[9] The book is not named after Naomi, but she is the character that holds the plot. Had Elimelech died before the famine hit Judah, it would not have mattered to the plot. In spite of the patriarchal legacy, the narrator does not present Naomi as a woman who depends on her husband. She stayed on in Moab with her sons even after Elimelech had died. In this regard, Elimelech is one of the flattest characters in the bible, an excess figure who lives in the narrative because of his name ("my God [is] king" or "my God kings;" אלי־מלך) rather than by his doing anything. His sons were more active. They at least took (the text does not say that they were "given") Moabite women as wives (Ruth 1:4), women whom Naomi appeared to have approved.

The book is named after one of Naomi's daughters-in-law, but the narrator's gaze favors Naomi's character and movements. The narrator's focalization followed Naomi from Bethlehem to Moab then back again. At the end of Ruth 1:1–5, there can be no doubt in any reader's mind that Naomi has taken hold of (or, taken over)[10] the plot. A story located at the time of the judges (Ruth 1:1) — implying that it was because of the judges that Bethlehem, of all places, because it is expected to be a "house of food," suffered a famine — is indeed Naomi's story.

---

[8] Compare Fewell and Gunn, *Compromising Redemption*, 25.
[9] There were no television then, or this story would have provided a catchy storyline for a *Crime Scene Investigation Unit* case.
[10] Compare with Yhwh taking over the plot in the story of Jonah. Cf. David M. Gunn and Danna Nolan Fewell, *Narrative in the Hebrew Bible* (New York: Oxford University Press, 1993), 132.

At the end of Ruth 1:1–5, the narrator again empties Naomi out. She has no husband or sons, and she is on her own in a foreign land. The narrator moved Naomi from one form of emptiness (famine in Bethlehem) to another form (widowhood and childlessness in Moab), as if to make room for Ruth. Naomi is however indispensable, for she is the one who brings Ruth to Judah.

Migration

The storyline—wife and husband made to leave their once stable home, along with children and household—is luring[11] and at once elusive.[12] Migration is a shared experience between Eve, Sarai and Hagar, Zipporah and Miriam, Vashti and the Queen of Sheba, and among those who are displaced and buried between the lines of biblical narratives, and many more who drowned in the whitewash of slavery and the waves of Polynesian navigation.[13] The causes of migration differ, as well as the potency of the forces that push people to move. Migration is not the same for all migrants, so it is unfair to romanticize the experience of migration. But the thrills and pains that come with migration are astonishing (albeit in differing degrees) for all migrants.

In the case of Naomi, the narrator is silent on how her family settled into Moab. Whose doors opened to them? Who gleaned in the fields of Moab to feed the family? Did they need to glean or were they privileged enough to buy their needs? How long did it take her family to take root in their new location? Did they feel that they belong, that they were at home, in Moab? The silence of the narrator on these lines of query gives the impression that their settlement was smooth. That says a lot about Naomi and her family. They had the resources and the skills to adapt (which are necessary for survival in a new land). That also says a lot

---

[11] A narrative constructs worlds and lives with words (language) that lure readers. Gunn and Fewell describe the attracting power of words/language as follows: "language lures us—allures us—from one word to another, from one meaning of a word to another, from the literal to the metaphorical, from one part of a text into another, from one text into another" (*Narrative in the Hebrew Bible*, 147).

[12] See my engagement with the elusive nature of language in *Elusions of Control: Biblical Law on the Words of Women* (Atlanta: Society of Biblical Literature; Leiden: Brill, 2003).

[13] I discuss the latter in "Migration and Mission Routes/Roots in Oceania," forthcoming in Elaine Padilla and Peter Phan, eds., *Christianities in Migration: The Global Perspective* (New York: Palgrave, forthcoming).

about Moab and its people (Naomi's new neighbors). They were open and hospitable.

The foregoing gleaning invites a change of views and of hearts for Naomi and for Moab and its people.[14] Moab does not come through in the narrative as a godforsaken place, and its people are not presented as inhospitable or ungenerous. Like Egypt in the Joseph cycle, Moab was a land of refuge. Moab and the Moabites should therefore not be straight-jacketed by the biases of racial and ethnic stereotypes.[15] Put another way, *'oua 'e 'omai e me'a mei tu'a ke tā-palasia'aki 'a Moape* (Tongan: "don't bring something from outside [of the narrative] to condemn Moab").

The passing of Elimelech soon upon the family's arrival suggests that either Naomi was well-endowed or she had to glean in order to feed her family. Her sons (בן) were not young men (נער),[16] so i do not expect them to be sent out to glean. As a single mother who was the head of her family, Naomi would have had to do a lot of stimulating behind the narrator's brief account in Ruth 1:3–4 to root her family in their new setting. She gleaned for more than grains, and Moab opened more than its doors to her and her sons. The marriage of the sons (Ruth 1:4) would have helped in establishing their roots in the new land. Nothing suggests welcome and homeliness as well as marriage does. Naomi's sons and their Moabite neighbors reached a point where they were comfortable with each other's bodies. Marriage can be political also, for profit and/or for control, and Naomi appears to have motivated things in Moab before the end of Ruth 1:4.

Migration makes people do new (and strange) tasks, think otherwise, and speak different languages. Migration takes one across

---

[14] The book of Numbers is especially harsh against Moab and its people, as in the stories of Balaam and his ass (Num 22–24) and of Baal-peor (Num 25). On Num 25, see Anthony Rees' *[Re]Reading Again: A Mosaic Reading of Numbers 25* (New York: Bloomsbury, 2015).

[15] I make a similar appeal on behalf of Esau, Edom and Edomites in "Releasing the Story of Esau from the Words of Obadiah," in *The Bible and the Hermeneutics of Liberation*, ed. Alejandro F. Botta and Pablo R. Andiñach (Atlanta: Society of Biblical Literature, 2009), 87–104.

[16] I am appealing here to the identification of the workers in Boaz's field as young men, from the Hebrew root נער (see e.g. Ruth 2:5), even though NJPS renders the plural form of this as "men" in Ruth 2:9 (as if young men are not capable of laboring in the field or of molesting women). The narrator does not give the age of Naomi's sons, but it makes a difference to me as a Pacific islander to have a sense of whether they could work in the fields or not. Were they old enough to glean and labor as one expects of נער? Whether they were younger or older than נער is up to the imagination and the experience of the reader.

cultural and linguistic borders and puts one (as migrant, foreigner) in a place of vulnerability. How do they do things in the new (strange) land that one has entered? How may we sing our songs (cf. Ps 137) and tell our songlines in the new land? What do the new neighbors value? What are they saying? What do they mean? How do we *not* offend them?

As a foreigner to Moab, Naomi would have been culturally and linguistically vulnerable. But she persevered and in time gained wisdom and became more savvy. She in fact survived for ten years as a foreigner and a widow in Moab (Ruth 1:4). Before Ruth 1:4 ends, she would have learned what it takes to survive and prosper in a foreign land. I imagine that she would have learned something about how Moabites think and do things, and so when she rose to return to Judah she was not simple-minded and uncultured. She was, for sure, a victim of the situation (famine and death), but she would not have been a pushover. No pushover would have decided to migrate to Moab and survived or easily decide to return to the people whom s/he abandoned. It takes courage to migrate and double that courage to return home. Part of the challenge for returning home (remigration) is relearning one's ways and people.

Time seems to speed up around Naomi. In four verses, the narrator accelerates the progress of events. Famine. Departure. Arrival. Marriage. Death. Widowhood. In-law-hood. In a matter of four verses, ten years pass by leaving three widows before the reader (Ruth 1:1–4). The death of the two sons is simultaneous, and loss increases threefold for Naomi (Ruth 1:5). The death of her three men, however, is not the reason why she decided to return to Judah. She returned for the food (Ruth 1:6), as we put it in Tongan, she returned because *na'e vaivai ki hono kete* ("she had weakness for her stomach"). Her children had passed, so she did not have crying mouths to feed. Did she rise to return only for the food? Was there something else in Judah that she wanted?

In my Tongan eyes, taking the initiative to secure food for oneself and for one's family—which we call *kai fa'o*, referring to ones who eat and at once pack food to take away—is both discouraged and admired. It is discouraged because as islanders we are a relational people, so we are expected to share (rather than look out only for one's own needs), and admired because we are a feasting people. Our cultures are nurtured around the sharing of food, and *kai fa'o* is what we do but say that we should not do. This is like readers who find fault in Eve picking from the fruit of the Tree of Knowing Good and Bad (Gen 2–3) and at the same time appreciate the freedom and enlightenment that resulted from her action. I would do the same if i were in her place. In fact, i would pick more than two fruits. Like the story of Eve, the story of Naomi twirls in the currents of *kai fa'o*. Naomi chased food to Moab and then back to Bethlehem.

With food come producers of food, who were men in Naomi's world, like the way it is in the village settings in Oceania. Products and producers were easily and closely associated then, unlike the way that stores and markets in recent times distance consumers from the farmers and the workers of the fields (so Koosed 2011). Produce did not grow in supermarkets in Naomi's world. In Moab and in Judah, people knew where food came from. Furthermore, food was associated with land, inheritance and blessing. S/he who has something to eat is blessed, for the land has been visited by fertility. Availability of food helped maintain peace among peoples, and distribution of food and resources was one of the areas at which justice was measured. Lack and availability of food was what made Naomi migrate to and from Moab, but food was one strand in an intricate weaving of many stuff. In this connection, if Naomi was a Tongan mother, i would argue that she was returning to Judah to glean and pack more than food. To *kai fa'o*? Yes! She had her eyes on the producers and on the land as well.

RETURN

Yhwh remembered, and food returned to Judah's storehouse. There was food in Moab still, but Judah was now piling up. Upon hearing of this return of fortune, Naomi rises to return for the home food, and she took the attention of the narrator with her. The story was not about her alone, but she is definitely the *tama'imata* (Tongan: "pupil") in the narrator's eyes. The narrator's attention remigrates with her. Moab is a turning point, a round-about, in the narrative. Naomi comes to Moab as if to off-load her husband and sons, then turns back to Bethlehem to reclaim and reestablish herself.

Daughters-in-law Ruth and Orpah began the journey with Naomi (Ruth 1:6–7). At first, she did not seem to mind their tagging along. Then God-knows-what happened, and Naomi tells the younger widows to return "each to her mother's house" (Ruth 1:8). It would have been damaging to Naomi's character had she told Orpah and Ruth "to stay" while they were still in Moab. That would portray Naomi as the one who is abandoning her daughters-in-law, as Yhwh did to Judah (causing the famine) and she and her family did to their Judean neighbors earlier in the story. In terms of her daughters-in-law, it was better that she sends them back after they departed the vicinities of their homes and away from the hearing of their relatives, for that would make Orpah and Ruth appear to be the ones who were abandoning Naomi. Abandonment seeps through the seams of this story, and who is seen to have abandoned whom depends on when and from where the daughters-in-law were returned to their homes.[17] Did it matter to Naomi how the other Moabites think of her?

There is a shift from *food* in Ruth 1:6 to *land* in Ruth 1:7. This shift suggests that Naomi's return was not just about food for her stomach but also about the land that is now fertile. Her dead husband owned a piece of the land that is now fertile, to which she has rights by marriage. Her sons' widows could claim the land, and that would be a problem seeing that she had not completely ruled out the possibility of taking another husband and bearing other sons (see Ruth 1:12). Should she acquire Elimelech's land, any future sons of hers would be endowed with land even if their father were landless. If this was the option she wanted, Orpah and Ruth would be in the way. It would be better for Naomi to return alone, as one widow rather than one of three widows who could claim Elimelech's land and inheritance. This helps explain why she did not want her daughters-in-law to arrive at Judah. They could claim the land and inheritance she wanted. They would not just be reminders of her past loss (i.e., husband and sons) but the cause of future loss (i.e., land and inheritance). Twice she sends them back, and she succeeded with Orpah after the second time,[18] but Ruth would not budge.

Nothing in the narrative bars Naomi from loving Ruth deeply and from wanting to send her home in order to protect her from the jibing she expected her old friends and relatives to dish out upon her arrival to Bethlehem. Ruth was young and inexperienced on crosscultural relations to know the stuff one cops when one returns home. The delight of homecoming is a fleeting experience. It is not long before welcome wanes, and one becomes the butt of the local people's jokes and

---

[17] The matter of abandonment feeds the exchange between Ruth and Naomi that ensued. After Naomi insisted the second time, Orpah kissed Naomi then she went back to her family. Ruth on the other hand persisted, committing to go all the way with Naomi, until death do them part (Ruth 1:9–17).

[18] Orpah chose the more difficult option, if read intertextually with the story of Tamar (Gen 38). She returned to her family as a widow, as used property, in a world where the ideal situation for a woman was to be married and to have children (which is one of the explanations for Tamar coming to wait for Judah at the crossing at Enaim). At her hometown, Orpah would be seen as a curse to any man who might be interested in her.

Orpah drops off the narrative, leaving one to imagine how she might react if she heard of the pleasures and fortunes that Ruth found later in the story. I imagine that she would have regretted not going back with Naomi.

derisions. *Fie pālangi* ("wannabe White," i.e., wannabe better),[19] she would be called.

Homecoming is celebrated in many legends (e.g., Homer's *Iliad*) and cultures, but this is not to say that all homes are settled, comforting, and uncontested (see e.g., Joshua and Judges). There are many conversations around "home" as real, ideological, desired, lived, and/or storied,[20] which i opt not to enter in this essay, but to simply interject that Naomi's return was to a home that was nebulous and troublesome. She had not been away long enough for memories (which are socially constructed) to die away. Naomi had living memories about her home and her people, and so did they about her. It is possible that these conditions (the living and endurance of memories) had something to do with her not wanting her daughters-in-law to return with her to Judah.

Naomi in this gleaning finds her match in Ruth. Naomi enters into the story and into Moab with a husband and two sons and returns to Judah a widow with a foreign woman at her side. She who abandoned the land to find food and refuge over the sea (Moab was across the sea from Judah) returns, and they who endured the famine would have been curious. A (prodigal) daughter of Beth-lehem was back without her men. Upon arrival, she stirs (תהה) the town. The local women ask, "Is this Naomi?" (1:19).

LOCALS

There are two sets of locals[21] in this narrative: the people of Moab and the people of Judah who did not migrate in order to escape the famine. Except for Orpah and Ruth, the locals of Moab are ignored, whereas the locals of Judah, who are differentiated according to age, gender, and

---

[19] This is similar to the cultural critique that South Korean artist PSY gives in his "Gangnam style" (Korean: 강남스타일). PSY pokes fun at people who pretend to be from Gangnam, a wealthy district in Seoul (on the south side of the Han river). PSY released "Gangnam Style" on 15 July 2012 as the lead single of his sixth studio album *PSY 6 (Six Rules), Part 1*. Wikipedia reports that as of 17 December 2012, the music video has been viewed over 969 million times on YouTube (http://en.wikipedia.org/wiki/Gangnam_Style).

[20] See for instance Sef Carroll's "Homemaking: Reclaiming the Ideal of Home as a Framework for Hosting Cultural and Religious Diversity," in *Colonial Contexts and Postcolonial Theologies: Storyweaving in the Asia-Pacific*, ed. Mark Brett and Jione Havea (New York: Palgrave, 2014), 219–29.

[21] I use "locals" here to refer to the people who belong to a place. They may not be indigenous to that place, but their roots are [from] there.

class, speak and perform in the story.[22] Older local Judean men are welcoming and hospitable even when they pass judgment (Ruth 4:11–12), and the older local women were excited and nurturing (Ruth 1:19; 4:14–17). The younger local men (Ruth 2:3, 9) and women (Ruth 2:8, 23; 3:2) of Judah, on the other hand, are employed but not heard.

When one reads the movements of Naomi, gleaning the story of Ruth with eyes that are attentive to the local peoples and their interests,[23] one finds bias against both sets of locals. The narrator gives no attention to the locals of Moab, and Naomi referred to but did not name the mothers of Orpah and Ruth to whose houses Naomi told Ruth and Orpah to return (Ruth 1:8). The houses of the two Moabite mothers are depicted as service counters to which unwanted or damaged goods may be returned. Naomi did not want exchange; only to return. Seen this way, what Naomi proposed is insulting to my Tongan eyes. She did not have the decency to accompany her daughters-in-law back to their mothers' houses, thank their mothers for raising them and for permitting them to be taken by her sons, and ask that they be received back, because her sons have passed away without giving children for the daughters, and she (Naomi) was returning to Judah. If Naomi had done so, she would be highly appreciated in Tongan circles. If Naomi had done so, i imagine that Ruth and Naomi might have agreed to return to their mothers' houses.

I read Naomi's action as lack of respect toward locals, but there is another reading, which suggests another form of disrespect. This is the reading suggested by Wil Gafney, who saw in the use of *ns'* (נשא, "to take"—as in "they took them as wives" in Ruth 1:4) as indication that Ruth and Orpah were "picked up" or abducted into marriage.[24] If "rape marriage" (which takes place in Gafney's as well as in my contexts) is how Orpah and Ruth came into Naomi's household, then this helps me

---

[22] The narrator was not interested in the locals of Moab, but one may assume that they were similar to the locals of Judah. They would be diverse and complex. Some would have questioned, confronted, and be antagonistic against Naomi, but some would have extended welcome, accommodation, and assistance.

[23] See e.g. my "Telling as if a Local: Toward Homing the Bible Outside Western [Main]Streams," *Joskiran: Journal of Religion and Thought* 5 (2008): 80–95 and "Local Lectionary Sites," in *Christian Worship in Australia: Inculturating the Liturgical Tradition,* ed. Anita Monro and Stephen Burns (Strathfield: St Pauls, 2009), 117–28.

[24] Wil Gafney, "Ruth," in *The Africana Bible: Reading Israel's Scriptures from Africa and the African Diaspora,* ed. Hugh R. Page Jr. et al. (Minneapolis: Fortress, 2010), 250 (249–54).

cope with why Naomi did not accompany her daughters-in-law to their mothers' houses. Naomi did not want to face the two Moabite mothers, because her sons had violated their daughters. Naomi would rather run away and forget about them, than face up to and compensate for the wrongs of her sons.

Both readings try to understand Naomi's action, and i assume that as mother-in-law she had a lot of authority over her daughters-in-law.[25] Because of the crosscultural makeup of the story, i also assume bias against [foreign] locals. On this note, it would help to cross-check:[26] Did Naomi [unconsciously] act the way she did, because she was biased against the locals of Moab? Are readers also biased against the locals of Moab? How may we glean this story so that we come to terms with our biases (esp. biases against the locals of Moab)?

Moab lost two daughters to Naomi and soon thereafter two sons-in-law to death. When Naomi decided to return to Judah, she tried to return Moab's daughters and thus cut herself free from Moab. But a trace of Moab, in the character of Ruth, a local woman, goes (like a thorn on the side) with her. The locals of Moab are therefore not erased from Naomi's story.

Naomi returned to Judah and found the locals excited: "the whole city buzzed with excitement over them" (Ruth 1:19β, NJPS). The women greeted her with a question that is open to interpretation: "Can this be Naomi?" Whether to hear the question with a tone of awe, disbelief, skepticism and/or sarcasm, depends on how one reads the story. For Naomi, there was something poignant about the local women's question so she corrects them: "Don't call me Naomi" (pleasantness). "Call me Mara" (bitterness). Then she offers a very critical theological observation: "Shaddai has made my lot very bitter.... Yhwh has brought me back empty.... Yhwh has testified against me (or: dealt harshly with me)" (Ruth 1:20–21). To modern ears, Naomi's bluntness is evidence of her distress. She has lost a lot, and she has the right to be bitter.

Naomi's statement did not gain a response. The local women went silent; whether in awe or disbelief, depends on how one gleans the story. For the local people in Judah who survived the famine, there would be

---

[25] Kwok Pui-lan, "Finding Ruth a Home: Gender, Sexuality, and the Politics of Otherness," in *Postcolonial Imagination and Feminist Theology* (Louisville: Westminster John Knox, 2005), 111 (100–21).

[26] Cf. Kyung Sook Lee, "Neo-Confucian Ideology in the Interpretation of the Book of Ruth: Toward a Cross-checking Hermeneutics," in *Korean Feminists in Conversation with the Bible, Church and Society*, ed. Kyung Sook Lee and Kyung Mi Park (Sheffield: Phoenix, 2011), 1–13.

nothing radical about Naomi's statement. They know what it means for Shaddai to make their lot very bitter, to empty them out, and to deal harshly with them. They survived what Naomi claimed, and i imagine some of them would be annoyed with Naomi for she was one of those who ran away, leaving them to face the wrath of Yhwh. I imagine that some of them would have been disgusted with Naomi. Why then did they not respond to Naomi? Why did they not put Naomi in her place?

In light of the reading proposed earlier that Naomi was a privileged woman before she left Bethlehem, some of the local women may have been silent out of fear. People with status, wealth, and power have the ability to silence local people with their mere presence. Along this line, the complete silence of the local women is indicative of Naomi's former glory. The local women dare not speak up against a powerful Naomi. She still wielded the power to shut people up. In this regard, were the local women silent or silenced? Silenced by whom? By Naomi and/or by the narrator?

I do not think there was only one kind of reaction by the local women of Judah, but their diverse opinions did not matter to the narrator. I see in the narrator's attitude toward these locals the same attitude toward local peoples in the Asia-Pacific. I am imposing my own experience upon the narrator, of course, but seeing that he showed the same attitude to the locals of Judah and to the locals of Moab suggests that the narrator too had issues with local peoples. Local peoples are insignificant, undeserving of attention and affection. On the other hand, the foreigners (Naomi in Moab) and the returnees (or remigrants, as Naomi was in Judah) are deserving of attention.

Stirring

As a narrative, the narrator is the prime stirrer in Ruth 1, migrating Naomi to and from Moab, causing a stir in Moab and later in Bethlehem upon her return. In public, Naomi stirred things up in ways that both silenced locals (Ruth 1:19) and pushed them to give her credit (Ruth 4:16–17). She stirred things up even when she was not in the eyes of harvesters (Ruth 2:22), threshers (Ruth 3:1–4), and elders. She is undoubtedly a stirring woman. In drawing attention to Naomi's stirrings, as a migrant to Moab and as a remigrant to Judah, i find elements in her story that stir me up. Most troublesome is the attitude towards local peoples, especially the ones who are ignored and muted.

A "culture of silence"[27] exists among and over against local peoples, which drive to silence and suppress them. This culture of silence contributes to why narrators and texts ignore local peoples. Readers and gleaners at scriptural fields (read: texts), on the other hand, are not obliged to honor and uphold the culture of silence. One way to break the culture of silence is to stir the plot up and to shake the foundations upon which biases against local peoples stand. "Stirring Naomi" therefore extends a double invitation: to glean for how Naomi stirs the plot and to glean in order to stir Naomi up for the sake of confronting the culture of silence at the underside of the story.

---

[27] See Paulo Freire, *Pedagogy of the Oppressed,* translated by Myra Bergman Ramos with an introduction by Donaldo Macedo (New York: Continuum, 2005), esp. 87–124. For Freire, the aim of education is to enable the oppressed to break through, by speaking up (dialogics) against, the cultures of silence that desensitize and suppress them.

BIBLIOGRAPHY

AAP. "Flight from Nauru Ends Pacific Solution." *Sydney Morning Herald*, 8 February 2008. http://news.smh.com.au/national/flight-from-nauru-ends-pacific-solution-20080208-1qww.html.

AAP. "Gillard Announces Malaysian Solution." *Sydney Morning Herald*, 7 May 2011. www.smh.com.au/national/gillard-announces-malaysian-solution-20110507-1ed0h.html.

Ahn, Yong-Sung. "For a Better Future in Korean Biblical Studies: Dialoguing within Myself in a Different Context." Pages 67–79 in *The Future of a Biblical Past: Envisioning Biblical Studies on a Global Key*. Edited by Roland Boer and Fernando R. Segovia. Atlanta: Society of Biblical Literature, 2012.

Ashcroft, Bill, Gareth Griffiths, and Helen Tiffin. *Post-Colonial Studies: The Key Concepts*. 2nd ed. London: Routledge, 2007.

Bailey, Randall C., Tat-siong Benny Liew, and Fernando F Segovia, eds. *They Were All Together in One Place? Toward Minority Biblical Criticism*. Atlanta: Society of Biblical Literature, 2009.

Barker, Paul A. *The Triumph of Grace in Deuteronomy: Faithless Israel, Faithful Yahweh in Deuteronomy*. Carlisle: Paternoster, 2004.

Bells, Alice Odgen. *Helpmates, Harlots, and Heroes: Women's Stories in the Hebrew Bible*. Louisville: Westminster John Knox, 2007.

Berlin, Adele. *Poetics and Interpretation of Biblical Narrative*. Sheffield: Almond, 1983.

Bernstein, Moshe J. "Two Multivalent Readings in the Ruth Narrative." *JSOT* 50 (1991): 17–20.

Berquist, Jon L. "Resistance and Accommodation in the Persian Empire." Pages 41–58 in *In the Shadow of Empire: Reclaiming the Bible as a History of Faithful Resistance*. Edited by Richard A. Horsley. Louisville: Westminster John Knox, 2008.

Bhabha, Homi K. *The Location of Culture*. London: Routledge, 1994.

———. *The Location of Culture*. 2nd edition. London: Routledge, 2004.

Black, James. "Ruth in the Dark: Folktale, Law and Creative Ambiguity in the Old Testament." *Literature and Theology* 5 (1991): 20–36.

Bledstein, Adrien J. "Female Companionships: If the Book of Ruth Were Written by a Woman." Pages 116–33 in *The Feminist Companion to Ruth*. Edited by Athalya Brenner. Sheffield: Sheffield Academic, 1993.

Block, Daniel I. *Judges, Ruth*. NAC 6. Nashville: Broadman & Holman, 1999.

Boer, Roland. "Caught in Between: Australian Biblical Studies between Asia, the Pacific, and the West." Pages 223–35 in *The Future of the Biblical Past: Envisioning Biblical Studies in a Global Key*. Edited by Roland Boer and Fernando F. Segovia. Atlanta: Society of Biblical Literature, 2012.

Braulik, Georg. "The Book of Ruth as Intra-Biblical Critique of the Deuteronomic Law." *AcT* 19 (1999): 1–20.

Brenner, Athalya. *The Israelite Woman: Social Role and Literary Type in Biblical Narrative.* Sheffield: Sheffield Academic, 1985.

———. "Naomi and Ruth." Pages 70–84 in *A Feminist Companion to Ruth.* Sheffield: Sheffield Academic, 1993.

———. "Naomi and Ruth: Further Reflections." Pages 140–44 in *A Feminist Companion to Ruth.* Edited by Athalya Brenner. Sheffield: Sheffield Academic, 1993.

———. "Ruth as Foreign Worker and the Politics of Exogamy." Pages 158–62 in *Ruth and Esther.* Edited by A. Brenner. Sheffield: Sheffield Academic, 1999.

Brett, Mark G. *Decolonizing God: The Bible in the Tides of Empire.* Sheffield: Sheffield Phoenix, 2008.

British Consulate-General Hong Kong. "British Nationality (Hong Kong) Act 1997." UK in Hong Kong. http://ukinhongkong.fco.gov.uk/en/help-for-british-nationals/living-in-hong-kong/ethnic-minorities/.

Botterweck, G. Johannes, and Helmer Ringgren, eds. *Theological Dictionary of the Old Testament.* Translated by John T. Willis et al. 8 vols. Grand Rapids: Eerdmans, 1974–2006.

Bush, Frederic William. *Ruth, Esther.* WBC 9. Waco, TX: Word, 1996.

Camp, Claudia V. *Wisdom and the Feminine in the Book of Proverbs.* Sheffield: JSOT Press, 1985.

Campbell, Edward F. *Ruth: A New Translation with Introduction, Notes and Commentary.* AB 7. Garden City: Doubleday, 1975.

Carmichael, Calum M. "'Treading' in the Book of Ruth." *ZAW* 92 (1980): 248–66.

Carrapiett, W. J. S. *Kachin Tribes of Burma: For the information of Officers of the Burma Frontier Service.* Rangoon: Government Printing & Stationery, 1929.

Carroll, Sef. "Homemaking: Reclaiming the Ideal of Home as a Framework for Hosting Cultural and Religious Diversity." Pages 219–29 in *Colonial Contexts and Postcolonial Theologies: Storyweaving in the Asia-Pacific.* Edited by Mark Brett and Jione Havea. New York: Palgrave, 2014.

Chan, Kenneth Ka-lok. "Taking Stock of One Country, Two Systems." Pages 44–49 in *"One Country, Two Systems" in Crisis: Hong Kong's Transformation Since the Handover.* Edited by Yiu-chung Wong. Lanham: Lexington Books, 2004.

Chan, Kin Man. "Cleavages and Challenges in Hong Kong's Pro-Democracy Camp." *Hong Kong Journal* 22 (2011): 2–3. http://www.hkjournal.org/PDF/2011_fall/3.pdf.

Cheung, Tony. "People Power Warns of Heavy Tactics to Get Its Point Across in Legco." *South China Morning Post,* 9 October 2012.

Chia, Philip. "On Naming the Subject: Postcolonial Reading of Daniel 1." *Jian Dao* 7 (1997): 17–36.

———. "Biblical Studies in a Rising Asia: An Asian Perspective on the Future of the Biblical Past." Pages 81–95 in *The Future of the Biblical Past: Envisioning Biblical Studies in a Global Key.* Edited by Roland Boer and Fernando F. Segovia. Atlanta: Society of Biblical Literature, 2012.

Childs, Peter Jean Jacques Weber, and Patrick Williams. *Post-Colonial Theory and Literatures: African, Caribbean and South Asian*. Trier: Wissenschaftlicher Verlag Trier, 2006.
Chirichigno, Gregory C. *Debt-Slavery in Israel and the Ancient Near East*. JSOTSup 141. Sheffield: JSOT, 1993.
Chittister, Joan. *The Story of Ruth: Twelve Moments in Every Woman's Life*. With art by John August Swanson. Grand Rapids: Eerdmans, 2000.
Christensen, Duane L. *Deuteronomy 21:10–34:12*. WBC 6B. Nashville: Thomas Nelson, 2002.
Chu, Julie L. C. "Returning Home: The Inspiration of the Role Dedifferentiation in the Book of Ruth for Taiwanese Women." *Semeia* 78 (1997): 47–53.
Clarke, Sarah. "Liberals Accused of Trying to Rewrite History." Australian Broadcasting Corporation. http://www.abc.net.au/lateline/content/2001/s422692.htm.
Clines, David J. A. *Job 1–20*. WBC. Waco, TX: Word, 1989.
Collins, John J. *The Bible after Babel: Historical Criticism in a Postmodern Age*. Grand Rapids: Eerdmans, 2005.
Coorey, Phillip. "Gillard on the Front Foot, Lurches to Right, But Team Rudd Not Beaten." *Sydney Morning Herald*, 20 August 2012. http://www.smh.com.au/ federal-politics/political-opinion/gillard-on-the-front-foot-lurches-to-right-but-team-rudd-not-beaten-20120819-24gf0.html.
Crowell, Bradley L. "Postcolonial Studies and the Hebrew Bible." *Currents in Biblical Research* 7 (2009): 217–44.
D'Sa, Francis X. "How Is It That We Hear, Each of Us, in Our Own Native Language? A Tentative Cross-cultural Reading of the Incarnation (John 1) and Avatara (Bhagavadgita 4)." Pages 123–46 in *Scripture, Community, and Mission: Essays in Honor of D. Preman Niles*. Edited by Philip L. Wickeri. Hong Kong: Christian Council of Asia; London: Council of World Missions, 2002.
Daide, *Da Dai Li Ji*. Changsha: The Commercial Press, 1937.
Davis, Ellen F. *Proverbs, Ecclesiastes, and the Song of Songs*. Louisville: Westminster John Knox, 2000.
DeSilva, David A. "Using the Master's Tools to Shore Up Another's House: A Postcolonial Analysis of 4 Maccabees." *JBL* 126 (2007): 99–127.
Donaldson, Laura E. "The Sign of Orpah: Reading Ruth through Native Eyes." Pages 130–44 in *Ruth and Esther*. Edited by Athalya Brenner. *A Feminist Companion to the Bible* 2/3. Sheffield: Sheffield Academic, 1999.
Dozeman, Thomas B. *Methods for Exodus*. Cambridge: Cambridge University Press, 2010.
Dube, Musa W. "Divining Ruth for International Relations." Pages 179–98 in *Other Ways of Reading: African Women and the Bible*. Edited by Musa W. Dube. Atlanta: Society of Biblical Literature, 2001.
Eskenazi, Tamara C. *In an Age of Prose: A Literary Approach to Ezra-Nehemiah*. Atlanta: Scholars Press, 1988.

Eskenazi, Tamara C., and Tikva Simone Frymer-Kensky. *Ruth*. JPS Bible Commentary. Philadephia: Jewish Publication Society, 2011.
Farmer, Kathleen A. *Who Knows What Is Good? A Commentary on the Books of Proverbs and Ecclesiastes*. Grand Rapids: Eerdmans, 1991.
Fewell, Danna N., and David M Gunn. 1989. "Boaz, Pillar of Society: Measures of Worth in the Book of Ruth." *JSOT* 45:45–59.
———. *Compromising Redemption: Relating Characters in the Book of Ruth*. Louisville: Westminster John Knox, 1990.
Fischer, Imtraud. "The Book of Ruth: A 'Feminist' Commentary to the Torah?" Pages 24–49 in *Ruth and Esther*. Edited by A. Brenner. Sheffield: Sheffield Academic, 1999.
Fishbane, Michael. *Biblical Interpretation in Ancient Israel*. Oxford: Clarendon, 1975.
Foskett, Mary F., and Jeffrey Kah-Jin Kuan, eds. *Ways of Being, Ways of Reading: Asian American Biblical Interpretation*. St. Louis: Chalice, 2006.
Freire, Paulo. *Pedagogy of the Oppressed*. Translated by Myra Bergman Ramos with an introduction by Donaldo Macedo. New York: Continuum, 2005.
Gafney, Wil. "Ruth." Pages 249–54 in *The Africana Bible: Reading Israel's Scriptures from Africa and the African Diaspora*. Edited by Hugh R. Page Jr. et al. Minneapolis: Fortress, 2010.
Gilhodes. *The Kachins: Religion and Custom*. 2nd edition. New Delhi: Mittal, 1995.
Gitay, Zefira. "Ruth and the Women of Bethlehem." Pages 82–183 in *The Feminist Companion to Ruth*. Edited by Athalya Brenner. Sheffield: Sheffield Academic, 1993.
Glover, Neil. "Your People, My People: An Exploration of Ethnicity in Ruth." *JSOT* 33 (2009): 302.
Goswell, Greg. "The Attitude to the Persians in Ezra-Nehemiah." *TJ* 32 (2011): 198–201.
———. "The Absence of a Davidic Hope in Ezra-Nehemiah." *TJ* 33 (2012): 19–31.
———. "The Book of Ruth and the House of David." *EvQ* 86 (2014): 116–129.
Goulder, Michael D. "Ruth: A Homily on Deuteronomy 22–25?" Pages 307–19 in *Of Prophets, Visions and Wisdom of Sages: Essays in Honour of R. Norman Whybray on his Seventieth Birthday*. Edited by Heather A. McKay and David J. A. Clines. JSOTSup 162. Sheffield: Almond, 1993.
Gow, Murray D. *The Book of Ruth: Its Structure, Theme and Purpose*. Leicester: Apollos, 1992.
———. "Ruth." Pages 176–78 in *New Dictionary of Biblical Theology*. Edited by T. Desmond Alexander and Brian S. Rosner. Leicester: InterVarsity, 2000.
Griffiths, Emma. "Immigration Minister Scott Morrison Defends Use of Term 'Illegal Arrivals,' Plays Down PNG Police Incident." http://www.abc.net.au/news/2013-10-21/immigration-minister-scott-morrison-defends-use-of-illegals-term/5035552.
Gunn, David M., and Danna Nolan Fewell. *Narrative in the Hebrew Bible*. New York: Oxford University Press, 1993.

Gutstein, Naphtali. "Proverbs 31:10–31: The Woman of Valor as Allegory." *Jewish Bible Quarterly* 27 (1999): 36–39.

Halton, Charles. "An Indecent Proposal: The Theological Core of the Book of Ruth." *SJOT* 26 (2012): 39.

Hanson, Ola. *The Kachin: Their Custom and Tradition.* New York: AMS, 1981.

Harm, Harry J. "The Function of Double Entendre in Ruth Three." *JOTT* 7 (1995): 23.

Harris, R. Laird, Gleason L. Archer Jr., and Bruce K. Waltke. *Theological Wordbook of the Old Testament.* 2 vols. Chicago: Moody Press, 1980.

Havea, Jione. "To Love Cain More Than God, in Other Words, 'Nody' Gen 4:1–16." Pages 91–112 in *Levinas and Biblical Studies.* Edited by Tamara C. Eskenazi, Gary A. Phillips, and David Jobling. Atlanta: Society of Biblical Literature, 2003.

———. *Elusions of Control: Biblical Law on the Words of Women.* Atlanta: Society of Biblical Literature; Leiden: Brill, 2003.

———. "Would the Real Native Please Sit Down!" Pages 199–210 in *Faith in a Hyphen: Cross-cultural Theologies Down Under.* Edited by Clive Pearson. Parramatta: UTC Publications; Openbook, 2004.

———. "Telling as if a Local: Toward Homing the Bible outside Western [Main]Streams." *Joskiran: Journal of Religion and Thought* 5 (2008): 80–95.

———. "Local Lectionary Sites." Pages 117–28 in *Christian Worship in Australia: Inculturating the Liturgical Tradition.* Edited by Anita Monro and Stephen Burns. Strathfield: St Pauls, 2009.

———. "Releasing the Story of Esau from the Words of Obadiah." Pages 87–104 in *The Bible and the Hermeneutics of Liberation.* Edited by Alejandro F. Botta and Pablo R. Andiñach. Atlanta: Society of Biblical Literature, 2009.

———. "Engaging Scriptures from Oceania." Pages 3–19 in *Bible, Borders, Belonging(s): Engaging readings from Oceania.* Edited by Jione Havea, David Neville, and Elaine Wainwright. Semeia Studies. Atlanta: Society of Biblical Literature, 2014.

———. "Migration and Mission Routes/Roots in Oceania." In *Christianities in Migration: The Global Perspective.* Edited by Elaine Padilla and Peter Phan. New York: Palgrave, forthcoming.

Hawkins, Tom R. "The Wife of Noble Character in Proverbs 31:10–31." *Bibliotheca Sacra* 153.609 (1996): 12–23.

Hoglund, Kenneth G. *Achaemenid Imperial Administration in Syria-Palestine and the Missions of Ezra and Nehemiah.* Atlanta: Scholars Press, 1992.

Holmstedt, Robert D. 2010. *Ruth: A Handbook on the Hebrew Text.* Waco, TX: Baylor University Press.

Hong Kong Connection. "14 Years On—The Hong Kong SAR." Radio Television Hong Kong. http://programme.rthk.org.hk/rthk/tv/programme.php?name=tv/hkce&d=2011-10-06&p=1981&e=154313&m=episode.

Hong Kong Institute of Asia-Pacific Studies. "Survey on How Hong Kong People Feel about the Status Quo after Handover to China since 1997 (2011)."

Chinese University of Hong Kong. http://www.cuhk.edu.hk/hkiaps/tellab/pdf/telepress/11/Press_Release_20110628.pdf.

Huang, Wei. "The Meaning of *h'lm* in Qoheleth 3:11 from a Chinese Perspective." Pages 103–110 in *Mapping and Engaging the Bible in Asian Cultures: Congress of the Society of Asian Biblical Studies 2008 Seoul Conference*. Edited by Yeong Mee Lee and Yoon Jong Yoo. Seoul: Christian Literature Society of Korea, 2009.

Hubbard Jr., Robert L. *The Book of Ruth*. The Book of Ruth. NICOT. Grand Rapids: Eerdmans, 1988.

Huddart, David. *Homi K. Bhabha*. London: Routledge, 2006.

IFJ Asia-Pacific. "Mainland Interference in Political Reporting Alleged in Hong Kong." *International Federation of Journalists*, March 22, 2012. http://asiapacific.ifj.org/en/articles/mainland-interference-in-political-reporting-alleged-in-hong-kong.

Ja, Kumje Roi. "Jiwoi Jiwa Ni A Prat Kaw Nna Wunpawng Shayi Num Sha Ni Hpe Makawp Maga Da Ai Ahkaw Ahkang Ni." *Buga Shanan*, 2005–2006. http://www.kachinnet.net/Article/2006/JanMarch/unpawng%20shayi%20num%20kasha%20ni%20hpe%20makawp%20maga%20da%20ai%20ahkaw%20ahkang.htm.

Japhet, Sara. "People and Land in the Restoration Period." Pages 96–116 in *From the Rivers of Babylon to the Highlands of Judah: Collected Studies on the Restoration Period*. Winona Lake: Eisenbrauns, 2006.

Kachin Baptist Convention. "A Short History and Formation of KBC" http://www.kbckachin.com/Page/KBC%20Bro.pdf.

Kalmin, Richard. "Levirate Law" [Heb. *Yibûm*]. *ABD* 4: 296–297.

Keita, Schadrac, and Janet W. Dyk. "The Scene at the Threshing Floor: Suggestive Readings and Intercultural Considerations on Ruth 3." *BT* 57 (2006): 17–32.

Kim, Yong-Bock. "The Bible among the Minjung of Korea: Kairotic Listening and Reading of the Bible." Pages 70–91 in *Scripture, Community, and Mission: Essays in Honor of D. Preman Niles*. Edited by Philip L. Wickeri. Hong Kong: Christian Council of Asia; London: Council of World Missions, 2002.

Kinukawa, Hisako. "'… And Your God My God': How We Can Nurture Openness to Other Faiths; Ruth 1:1–19 Read from a Feminist Perspective of a Multi-Faith Community." Pages 193–208 in *Scripture, Community, and Mission: Essays in Honor of D. Preman Niles*. Edited by Philip L. Wickeri. Hong Kong: Christian Council of Asia; London: Council of World Missions, 2002.

Koehler, Ludwig, Walter Baumgartner, and Johann J. Stamm. *The Hebrew and Aramaic Lexicon of the Old Testament*. 3rd ed. Leiden: Brill, 1995, 2004.

Koosed, Jennifer L. *Gleaning Ruth: A Biblical Heroine and Her Afterlives*. Columbia: The University of South Carolina Press, 2011.

Kstes, Judith A., and Reimer, Gail Twersky, eds. *Reading Ruth: Contemporary Jewish Women Reclaim a Sacred Story*. New York: Ballantine, 1994.

Kwok, Pui-lan. "Postcolonialism, Feminism and Biblical Interpretation." Pages 261–76 in *Scripture, Community, and Mission: Essays in Honor of D. Preman*

Niles. Edited by Philip L. Wickeri. Hong Kong: Christian Council of Asia; London: Council of World Missions, 2002.

———. "Finding a Home for Ruth: Gender, Sexuality, and the Politics of Otherness." Pages 137–56 in *New Paradigms for Bible Study: The Bible in the Third Millennium.* Edited by Robert M. Fowler, Edith Blumhofer, and Fernando F. Segovia. New York: T&T Clark, 2004.

———. *Postcolonial Imagination and Feminist Theology.* Louisville: Westminster John Knox, 2005.

Kwon, Oh-Young. "1 Corinthians 12:12–13: An Ethnic Analysis and Its Evaluation from a Korean-Ethnocentric (*danil minjok*) Christian Context." Pages 123–39 in *Mapping and Engaging the Bible in Asian Cultures: Congress of the Society of Asian Biblical Studies 2008 Seoul Conference.* Edited by Yeong Mee Lee and Yoon Jong Yoo. Seoul: Christian Literature Society of Korea, 2009.

LaCocque, André. *The Feminine Unconventional: Four Subversive Figures in Biblical Tradition.* Minneapolis: Fortress, 1990.

———. *Ruth.* Translated by K. C. Hanson. Minneapolis: Fortress, 2004.

Lau, Peter H. W. "Gentile Incorporation into Israel in Ezra–Nehemiah?" *Bib* 90 (2009): 356–73.

———. *Identity and Ethics in the Book of Ruth: A Social Identity Approach.* BZAW 416. Berlin: de Gruyter, 2011.

Leach, Edmund R. *Political Systems of Highland Burma: A Study of Kachin Social Structure.* LSEMSA 44. London: Athlone Press, 1954.

Lee, Archie C. C. "Polyphonic Voices in the Bible." Pages 177–92 in *Scripture, Community, and Mission: Essays in Honor of D. Preman Niles.* Edited by Philip L. Wickeri. Hong Kong: Christian Council of Asia; London: Council of World Missions, 2002.

———. "The Bible in Asia: Contesting and Contextualizing." Pages 19–35 in *Mapping and Engaging the Bible in Asian Cultures: Congress of the Society of Asian Biblical Studies 2008 Seoul Conference.* Edited by Yeong Mee Lee and Yoon Jong Yoo. Seoul: Christian Literature Society of Korea, 2009.

Lee, Eunny. "Ruth, Book of." Pages 865–68 in *The New Interpreter's Dictionary of the Bible.* Edited by K. D. Sakenfeld. Vol. 4. Nashville: Abingdon, 2009.

Lee, Kyung Sook. "Neo-Confucian Ideology in the Interpretation of the Book of Ruth: Toward a Cross-checking Hermeneutics." Pages 1–13 in *Korean Feminists in Conversation with the Bible, Church and Society.* Edited by Kyung Sook Lee and Kyung Mi Park. Sheffield: Sheffield Phoenix, 2011.

Lee, Yeong Mee, and Yoon Jong Yoo, eds. *Mapping and Engaging the Bible in Asian Cultures: Congress of the Society of Asian Biblical Studies 2008 Seoul Conference.* Seoul: Christian Literature Society of Korea., 2009.

Levine, Amy-Jill. "Ruth." Pages 84–90 in *Women's Bible Commentary.* Edited by Carol A. Newsom and Sharon H. Ringe. Expanded ed. Louisville: Westminster John Knox, 1998.

Li, Chichang. "Returning to China : Biblical Interpretation in Postcolonial Hong Kong." *Biblical Interpretation* 7 (1999): 156–73.

Liew, Tat-siong Benny. *What Is Asian American Biblical Hermeneutics? Reading the New Testament.* Honolulu: University of Hawaii Press, 2008.

Linafelt, Tod, and Timothy K. Beal. *Ruth and Esther, Berit Olam.* Edited by David W. Cotter. Studies in Hebrew Narrative and Poetry. Collegeville, MN: Liturgical Press, 1999.

Lyn, Tan Ee, and James Pomfret. "Crowds Protest in Hong Kong as Hu Anoints Leader." *Reuters*, 2 July 2012. http://in.reuters.com/article/2012/07/02/hongkong-china-idINDEE86102Y20120702.

Lyons, Ellen Louise. "A Note on Proverbs 31:10–31." Pages 241–42 in *The Listening Heart: Essays in Wisdom and the Psalms in Honor of Roland E. Murphy.* Edited by Kenneth G. Hoglund et. al. Sheffield: JSOT Press, 1987.

Masenya, Madipoane. "Proverbs 31:10–31 in a South African Context: A Reading for the Liberation of African (Northern Sotho) Women." *Semeia* 78 (1997): 56–68.

———. "Ruth." Pages 86–91 in *Global Bible Commentary.* Edited by Daniel Patte. Nashville: Abingdon, 2004.

———. "Struggling with Poverty/Emptiness: Rereading the Naomi-Ruth Story in African-South Africa." *Journal of Theology for Southern Africa* 120 (2004): 46–50.

Matthews, Victor H. *Judges/Ruth.* NCBC. Cambridge: Cambridge University Press, 2004.

McCreesh, Thomas P. "Wisdom as Wife: Proverbs 31: 10–31." *Revue Biblique* 92 (1985): 25–46.

McKane, William. *Proverbs: A New Approach.* Philadelphia: The Westminster Press, 1970.

Melanchthon, Monica Jyotsna. "Dalit Reading of Genesis 10–11:9." Pages 161–76 in *Scripture, Community, and Mission: Essays in Honor of D. Preman Niles.* Edited by Philip L. Wickeri. Hong Kong: Christian Council of Asia; London: Council of World Missions, 2002.

———. "Unleashing the Power Within: The Bible and Dalits." Pages 49–65 in *The Future of a Biblical Past: Envisioning Biblical Studies on a Global Key.* Edited by Roland Boer and Fernando R. Segovia. Atlanta: Society of Biblical Literature, 2012.

Mettinger, Tryggve N. D. *In Search of God: The Meaning and Message of the Everlasting Names.* Translated by Frederick H. Cryer. Philadelphia: Fortress, 1988.

Meyers, Carol L. "Everyday Life: Women in the Period of the Hebrew Bible." Pages 244–51 in *Women's Bible Commentary.* Edited by Carol A. Newsom and Sharon H. Ringe. Louisville: Westminster John Knox Press, 1992.

———, ed. *Women in Scripture.* Grand Rapids: Eerdmans, 2000.

Miles, Johnny. "The 'Enemy Within': Refracting Colonizing Rhetoric in Narratives of Gibeonite and Japanese Identity." Pages 129–68 in *Postcolonialism and the Hebrew Bible: The Next Step.* Edited by Roland Boer. Atlanta: Society of Biblical Literature, 2013.

Milgrom, Jacob. *Leviticus 23–27.* AB 3B. New York: Doubleday, 2000.

Miller, Patrick D. *They Cried to the Lord: The Form and Theology of Biblical Prayer.* Minneapolis: Fortress, 1994.
Murphy, Roland E. *Proverbs.* World Biblical Commentary. Edited by Bruce M. Metzger et.al. Nashville: Thomas Nelson, 1998.
Murphy, Roland E., and Elizabeth Huwiler. *Proverbs, Ecclesiastes, Song of Songs.* New International Biblical Commentary. Peabody, MA: Hendrickson, 1999.
Nadar, Sarojini. "A South African Indian Womanist Reading of the Character of Ruth." Pages 159–75 in *Other Ways of Reading: African Women and the Bible.* Edited by Musa W. Dube. Atlanta: Society of Biblical Literature, 2001.
Nicholson, Ernest W. "The Meaning of the Expression עם הארץ in the Old Testament." *JSS* 10 (1965): 59–66.
Nielsen, Kirsten. *Ruth: A Commentary.* Translated by Edward Broadbridge. Louisville: Westminster John Knox, 1997.
Niles, Damayanthi M. A. "Whose Text Is It Anyway? How Text Functions to Build Identity and Community." Pages 304–14 in *Scripture, Community, and Mission: Essays in Honor of D. Preman Niles.* Edited by Philip L. Wickeri. Hong Kong: Christian Council of Asia; London: Council of World Missions, 2002.
O'Connor, Kathleen M. *The Wisdom Literature.* Collegeville: Liturgical Press, 1988.
Pa, Anna May Say. "Reading Ruth 3:1–5 from an Asian Woman's Perspective." Pages 47–59 in *Engaging the Bible in a Gendered World: An Introduction to Feminist Biblical Interpretations in Honor of Katherine Doob Sakenfeld.* Edited by Linda Day and Carolyn Pressler. Louisville: Westminster John Knox, 2006.
"Pacific Solution." Wikipedia. http://en.wikipedia.org/wiki/Pacific_Solution.
Pardes, Ilana. *Countertraditions in the Bible.* Cambridge: Harvard University Press, 1992.
Pattel-Gray, Anne. *Through Aboriginal Eyes: The Cry from the Wilderness.* Geneva: WCC, 1991.
Perdue, Leo G. *Proverbs.* Interpretation: A Bible Commentary for Teaching and Preaching. Louisville: John Knox, 2000.
Phillips, Anthony. "The Book of Ruth: Deception and Shame." *JJS* 37 (1986): 1–17.
Phillips, Janet. "The 'Pacific Solution' Revisited: A Statistical Guide to the Asylum Seeker Caseloads on Nauru and Manus Island." Parliment of Australia. http://www.aph.gov.au/About_Parliament/Parliamentary_Departments/Parliamentary_Library/pubs/BN/2012-2013/PacificSolution.
Pieris, Aloysius. "Cross-Scripture Reading in Buddhist-Christian Dialogue: A Search for the Right Method." Pages 229–50 in *Scripture, Community, and Mission: Essays in Honor of D. Preman Niles.* Edited by Philip L. Wickeri. Hong Kong: Christian Council of Asia; London: Council of World Missions, 2002.
Raja, Maria Arul. "Breaking Hegemonic Boundaries: An Intertextual Reading of the Madurai Veeran Legend and Mark's Story of Jesus." Pages 251–60 in *Scripture, Community, and Mission: Essays in Honor of D. Preman Niles.* Edited by Philip L. Wickeri. Hong Kong: Christian Council of Asia; London: Council of World Missions, 2002.

Rao, Naveen. "The Book of Ruth as a Clandestine Scripture to Sabotage Persian Colonial Agenda: A Paradigm for a Liberative Dalit Scripture." *Bangalore Theological Forum* 41 (2009): 114–34.

Rashkow, Ilona. "Ruth: The Discourse of Power and the Power of Discourse." Pages 26–41 in *A Feminist Companion to Ruth*. Edited by Athalya Brenner. Sheffield: Sheffield Phoenix, 1993.

Rees, Anthony. *[Re]Reading Again: A Mosaic Reading of Numbers 25*. New York: Bloomsbury, 2015.

Rogerson, John W. *A Theology of the Old Testament: Cultural Memory, Communication, and Being Human*. Minneapolis: Fortress, 2010.

Rongpei, Wang, trans. *A Pair of Peacocks to the Southeast Fly*. In *300 Early Chinese Poems (206 B.C.–A.D. 618)*. Changsha: Hunan People's Publishing House, 2006.

Said, Edward W. *Orientalism*. London: Penguin, 2003.

Sakenfeld, Katharine Doob. *Ruth*. Interpretation: A Bible Commentary for Teaching and Preaching. Louisville: John Knox, 1999.

———. *Just Wives? Stories of Power and Survival in the Old Testament and Today*. Louisville: Westminster John Knox Press, 2003.

Sals, Ulrike. "The Hybrid Story of Balaam (Numbers 22–24): Theology for the Diaspora in the Torah." *Biblical Interpretation* 16 (2008): 315–35.

Sassoon, Jack M. *Ruth: A New Translation with a Philological Commentary and a Formalist-Folklorist Interpretation*. 2nd edition. Sheffield: Sheffield Academic, 1989.

Saysell, Csilla. "Deuteronomy in the Intermarriage Crises in Ezra-Nehemiah." Pages 197–208 in *Interpreting Deuteronomy: Issues and Approaches*. Edited by David G. Firth and Philip S. Johnston. Nottingham: IVP, 2012.

Scott, James George. *Burma and Beyond*. London: Grayson, 1932.

Segovia, Fernando F. "Postcolonial and Diasporic Criticism in Biblical Studies: Focus, Parameters, Relevance." *Studies in World Christianity* 5 (1999): 177–95.

Segovia, Fernando F. and Mary Ann Tolbert, eds. *Teaching The Bible: The Discourses and Politics of Biblical Pedagogy*. Maryknoll: Orbis, 1998.

Shanahan, Dennis. "PM Lurches in Bid to Right Labor's Ship." *The Australian*. 20 July 2013. http://www.theaustralian.com.au/opinion/columnists/pm-lurches-in-bid-to-right-labors-ship/story-e6frg75f-1226682255779#.

Smith, Mark S. "'Your People Shall Be My People': Family and Covenant in Ruth 1:16–17." *CBQ* 69 (2007): 242–58.

Smith-Christopher, Daniel L. "The Mixed Marriage Crisis in Ezra 9–10 and Nehemiah 13: A Study of the Sociology of the Post-Exilic Judean Community." Pages 243–65 in *Second Temple Studies*. Edited by Tamara C. Eshkenazi and Kent Richards. JSOTSup 175. Atlanta: Scholars Press, 1994.

———. *A Biblical Theology of Exile*. Minneapolis: Fortress, 2002.

Spivak, Gayatri Chakravorty. *Other Asias*. Malden: Blackwell, 2008.

———. "Nationalism and the Imagination." *Lectora* 15 (2009): 75–98.

Stanton, Elizabeth C. "The Book of Ruth." Pages 20–25 in *A Feminist Companion to Ruth*. Edited by Athalya Brenner. Sheffield: Sheffield Academic, 1993.

Sugirtharajah, R. S. ed. *The Postcolonial Bible*. Sheffield: Sheffield Academic, 1998.
———. *Asian Biblical Hermeneutics and Postcolonialism: Contesting the Interpretations*. New York: Maryknoll, 1998.
———, ed. *Voices from the Margins: Reading the Bible in the Third World*. Revised and expanded 3rd ed. New York: Maryknoll, 2006.
———, ed. *Still at the Margins: Biblical Scholarship Fifteen Years after Voices from the Margin*. New York: T&T Clark, 2008.
———. *The Bible and Asia: From the Pre-Christian Era to the Postcolonial Age*. Cambridge: Harvard University Press, 2013.
Suqing, Lin. "Behind the Conflicts of Mother and Daughter-in-Law: An Explanation on the Marriage Tragedy of A Pair of Peacocks to the Southeast Fly and Phoenix Hairpin." *Writer Magazine* 5 (2008): 153.
Swarup, Paul. "The Bible in the Context of Multi-Textual Communities: A Study of Pandita Ramabai's Response (1858–1922)." Pages 204–222 in *Scripture, Community, and Mission: Essays in Honor of D. Preman Niles*. Edited by Philip L. Wickeri. Hong Kong: Christian Council of Asia; London: Council of World Missions, 2002.
Tate, W. Randolph, 2008. *Biblical Interpretation: An Integrated Approach*. 3rd edition. Peabody: Hendrickson.
Taylor, F. J. "Redeem" in TWB. Edited by Alan Richardson. New York: Macmillan, 1964.
Tegenfeldt, Herman. *A Century Growth: The Kachin Baptist Church of Burma*. South Pasadena, CA: The William Carey Library, 1913.
Tesoo, Yim. "Interpretation of the Law and the Gospel in Exodus from the Perspective of Minjung Theology." Pages 89–102 in *Mapping and Engaging the Bible in Asian Cultures: Congress of the Society of Asian Biblical Studies 2008 Seoul Conference*. Edited by Yeong Mee Lee and Yoon Jong Yoo. Seoul: Christian Literature Society of Korea, 2009.
The Economist Group. "Elections in Hong Kong: Functionally Democratic." *The Economist*. June 24, 2010. http://www.economist.com/node/16439175.
The Midrash Rabbah. New Compact ed. Vol. 4. London: Soncino Press, 1977.
Thiselton, Anthony C. "'Behind' and 'In Front of' the Text: Language, Reference and Indeterminancy" in *After Pentecost: Language and Biblical interpretation*. Edited by Craig Bartholomew, Colin Greene, and Karl Möller. Scripture and Hermeneutics 2. Carlisle: Paternoster, 2001.
Timmer, Daniel C. "The Intertextual Jonah face à l'empire: The Post-colonial Significance of the Book's Cotexts and Purported Neo-Assyrian Context." *JHS* 9 (2009): 1–22.
———. *A Gracious and Compassionate God: Mission, Salvation and Spirituality in the Book of Jonah*. NSBT. Nottingham: Apollos, 2011.
Torn, Susan Reimer. "Ruth Reconsidered." Pages 345–46 in *Reading Ruth: Contemporary Women Reclaim a Sacred Story*. Edited by Judith A. Kates and Gail T. Reimer. New York: Ballantine, 1994.
Tran, Mai-Anh Le. "Lot's Wife, Ruth, and Tô Thị: Gender and Racial Representation in a Theological Feast of Stories." Pages 123–36 in *Ways of*

Being, Ways of Reading: Asian American Biblical Interpretation. Edited by Mary F. Foskett and Jeffrey Kah-Jin Kuan. St. Louis: Chalice, 2006.

Trible, Phyllis. *God and the Rhetoric of Sexuality*. Philadelphia: Fortress, 1978.

———. "A Human Comedy." Pages 161–90 in *God and the Rhetoric of Sexuality*. Edited by K. R. R. Gros Louis and J. S. Ackerman. Literary Interpretations of Biblical Narratives 2. Nashville: Abingdon, 1982.

Trieu, Rosa. "Hongkongers' Press Freedom Threatened by China's Creeping Influence." *Forbes*, 25 June 2012. http://www.forbes.com/sites/rosatrieu/2012/06/25/hongkongers-press-freedom-threatened-by-chinas-creeping-influence/2/.

van Wolde, Ellen. "Texts in Dialogue with Texts: Intertextuality in the Ruth and Tamar Narratives." *BibInt* 5 (1977): 1–27.

———. *Ruth and Naomi*. London: SCM, 1997.

von Rad, Gerhard. *Deuteronomy: A Commentary*. Translated by Dorothea Barton. London: SCM Press, 1966.

Walker, Ting. "The High Court Decision on the Malaysian Solution." Australian Capital Territory. 25 November, 2011. http://www.abc.net.au/local/stories/2011/11/23/3374312.htm.

Waltke, Bruce K. *The Book of Proverbs: Chapters 15-31*. NICOT. Edited by R. K. Harrison and Robert L. Hubbard, Jr. Grand Rapids: Eerdmans, 2005.

Wang, Tai Il. "Performing the Scripture: Understanding the Bible from Korean Biblical Hermeneutics." Pages 37–52 in *Mapping and Engaging the Bible in Asian Cultures: Congress of the Society of Asian Biblical Studies 2008 Seoul Conference*. Edited by Yeong Mee Lee, and Yoon Jong Yoo. Seoul: Christian Literature Society of Korea, 2009.

Weems, Renita J. *Just A Sister Away*. Revised and updated. West Bloomfield: Warner, 2005.

Weinfeld, Moshe. "Ruth, Book of." In *Encyclopaedia Judaica*. Jerusalem: Keter, 1996.

Wickeri, Philip L. ed. *Scripture, Community, and Mission: Essays in Honor of D. Preman Niles*. Hong Kong: Christian Council of Asia; London: Council of World Missions, 2002.

Williamson, H. G. M. *Ezra, Nehemiah*. Waco, TX: Word, 1985.

Wolters, Albert M. "Proverbs 31:10–31 as Heroic Hymn: A Form-Critical Analysis." *VT* 38 (1988): 446–57.

Wong, Wai Ching. "Identity in Hybridity: Ruth in the Genealogy of Jesus: Matthew 1:1–17; Ruth 1–4." *Theologies and Cultures* 6 (2009): 98–109.

Yamaguchi, Satoko. "From Dualistic Thinking toward Inclusive Imagination." Pages 53–71in *Mapping and Engaging the Bible in Asian Cultures: Congress of the Society of Asian Biblical Studies 2008 Seoul Conference*. Edited by Yeong Mee Lee and Yoon Jong Yoo. Seoul: Christian Literature Society of Korea, 2009.

Yee, Gale A. "Yin/Yang Is Not Me: An Exploration into an Asian American Biblical Hermeneutics." Pages 152–63 in *Ways of Being, Ways of Reading: Asian American Biblical Interpretation*. Edited by Mary F. Foskett and Jeffrey Kah-Jin Kuan. St. Louis: Chalice, 2006.

Yoder, Christine Roy. "The Woman of Substance (אשת־חיל): A Socioeconomic Reading of Proverbs 31:10–31." *JBL* 122 (2003): 427–47.
Zakovitch, Yair. *Ruth: Introduction and Commentary*. Mikra le-Yisrael. Tel Aviv: Am Oved, 1990.
——. *Das Buch Rut: Ein jüdischer Kommentar*. Translated by Andreas Lehnardt. SBS 177. Stuttgart: Katholisches Bibelwerk, 1999.
Zevit, Ziony. "Dating Ruth: Legal, Linguistic and Historical Observations." *ZAW* 117 (2005): 574–600.
Ziegler, Yael. "'So Shall God Do...': Variations of an Oath Formula and Its Literary Meaning." *JBL* 126 (2007): 59–81.

CONTRIBUTORS

Elaine W. F. Goh is Malaysian Chinese raised in Penang, Malaysia. She is a Lecturer in Old Testament Studies at Seminari Theoloji Malaysia (STM) and was involved in pastoral ministry with the Methodist Church in Malaysia for seven years. She holds a Bachelor in Mass Communication (Universiti Sains Malaysia), Master of Divinity (STM), Master of Theology (Princeton Theological Seminary), and Doctor of Theology (South East Asia Graduate School of Theology/ATESEA Theological Union). Her area of research is Old Testament wisdom literature. Her most recent book is *Wisdom of Living in a Changing World: Readings from Ecclesiastes* (STM and Genesis, 2013).

Jione Havea is a native Methodist pastor from Tonga who is Primary Researcher at the Public and Contextual Theology Research Centre, Charles Sturt University (Australia). Jione has been gleaning around the story of Ruth for some time, most recently in "Bare Feet Welcome: Redeemer Xs Moses @ Enaim," in *Bible, Borders, Belonging(s): Engaging Readings in Oceania* (Society of Biblical Literature, 2014). Jione enjoys writing and editing as "threshing floor" experiences.

Peter H. W. Lau was born in Hong Kong but grew up in Australia. He holds an MDiv from Sydney Missionary and Bible College (SMBC) and a PhD from the University of Sydney, where he is an Honorary Associate. He previously taught at SMBC and is currently lecturing at Seminari Theoloji Malaysia (since 2010). He has published two books on Ruth: *Identity and Ethics in the Book of Ruth: A Social Identity Approach* (de Gruyter, 2011) and *The Book of Ruth: Risky Kindness* (Genesis, 2012). He is working on another book on Ruth from a biblical theology perspective.

Yan Lin was born in Xinjiang Uygur Autonomous Regions of China, but she is a Han. She is now teaching biblical studies and foreign literature in the College of Arts, Shenzhen University (China). She has published a book on Genesis, *Re-Reading Genesis 1–3 in the Light of Chinese Creation Myths* (2008). She has also translated *Introduction to the Hebrew Bible*, which was written by Barry Bandstra.

Surekha Nelavala is a pastor serving at ELCA. Nelavala has a PhD in Biblical Studies, New Testament, from Drew University, NJ, with several years of teaching experience in India and in United States. Nelavala has authored two books and published several articles internationally and has delivered lectures at several academic and church forums that include United Nations, World Council of Churches, and Lutheran World Federation on the topics related to religion, church, and social justice. Nelavala has cultivated intercultural and intercontextual perspectives as a biblical scholar. She is committed to the ecclesiological cause of bringing scholarship and people of God together in developing praxis-oriented liberating hermeneutics of the Bible, which she uses effectively in her ministry.

Roi Nu was born in Myanmar and holds a BA from Mandalay University, an MDiv from the Myanmar Institute of Theology, and an MTheol from the Divinity School of Chung Chi College, Hong Kong. She is now a lecturer at the Kachin Theological College, in Kutkai, Myanmar.

Anthony Rees is a Lecturer in Biblical Studies at United Theological College within the School of Theology, Charles Sturt University, and a research fellow of the Centre for Public and Contextual Theology, also at Charles Sturt University. His first book, *[Re]Reading Again*, a revision of his doctoral thesis, is published with T&T Clark/Bloomsbury, and a second, *Voices of the Wilderness*, the Numbers volume of the Earth Bible Commentary (Sheffield Phoenix Press) will appear in 2015. An advocate of multidisciplinary engagement, future publications will explore the intersection of postcolonial and ecological hermeneutics and the concept of music as biblical interpretation.

Sin Lung Tong is an adjunct lecturer at Ecclesia Bible College, Hong Kong. He has also taught at the Chinese Mission Seminary, Hong Kong and the Macau Bible Institute. He holds an MDiv from the Divinity School of Chung Chi College, the Chinese University of Hong Kong, and a MA(TS) from Princeton Theological Seminary, United States. He is particularly interested in reading the Old Testament narratives from a postcolonial perspective.

ANCIENT TEXTS INDEX

HEBREW BIBLE / OLD TESTAMENT

Genesis
2–3	117
3:6	21
3:17–19	112
4	112 n.5
4:1–16	112 n.5
6–9	112 n. 5
9:25	65, 68
10–11:9	11 n. 43, 132
11	112 n. 5
11:31–12:1	29
12:1–9	24
12:3	29
12:6b	112
12:10	21 n. 23, 112
14:16	65
19	113 n. 7
19:30–37	75
19:30–38	19, 24, 24 n. 30, 114
24:12–27	26
24:26–27	26
26:35	47 n. 2
27:46–28:5	21
29–30	24, 24 n. 33
29:15	65
38	20, 24, 47 n. 2, 57, 62, 119 n. 18
38:8	62, 63
38:14b	63
43:25	26 n. 40
50:20	29
50:24	26 n. 41

Exodus
2:11	4, 65, 68
4:31	26 n. 41
20:5	26 n. 41
22:22–24	18
23:10–11	31

Leviticus
19:9–10	18, 42
23–27	20 n. 21, 132
23:22	18
25	31 n. 63
25:8–55	31
25:23–25	20
25:24–34	64
25:25–34	64
25:47–54	64
25:47–55	64
25:48	64
25:48–49	20 n. 21
26:19–29	21

Numbers
14:18	26 n. 41
16:10	65, 68
21:29	51
22–24	38 n. 12, 40, 116 n. 14
22–25	21
24:18	73
25	116 n. 14
25:1–3	19, 40
25:6	68

Deuteronomy
5:9–10	26 n. 41
6:9	36
7	31 n. 62
7:1–4	19
7:3–4	27, 31 n. 60
10:18	18
14:29	18
15:1–6	31
16:11	18
17:14–20	33

Deuteronomy (cont.)	
23:3	40
23:3–6	19, 31 n. 62
24:19–21	18
24:19–22	42
25:5	49, 62, 63
25:5–10	20, 57, 61, 62, 65, 66, 67, 70, 71, 72
25:6	63
25:7	62, 63, 66
25:7–9	66
25:9	62, 63, 70
25:9–10	66
27:20	28 n. 50
28:23–24	21
28:38–42	21
30:1–5	22
30:6	23 n. 25

Joshua	120

Judges	120, 121
3:12–20	21
10:6	21
11:24	51
14:5	65, 68
14:15–20	22
17:1–4	80 n. 22
19	113 n. 7

Ruth	
1	1, 3, 111
1–4	6 n. 19
1:1	21 n. 23, 105, 112, 114
1:1–2	21, 113
1:1–4	117
1:1–5	114, 115
1:1–19	13 n. 53
1:2b	21
1:3	114
1:3–4	116
1:4	114, 116, 117, 121
1:5	117
1:6	22, 26, 105, 111, 113, 117, 119
1:7	22, 119
1:8	22, 23, 118, 121
1:8–9	27, 28, 36
1:10	22
1:11	22
1:11–13	36, 49
1:12	22, 117
1:13	26, 49
1:14	106
1:15	22, 23, 36, 62, 63
1:16	19 n. 14, 22, 106
1:16–17	12, 22, 31 n. 60, 35, 36–37, 36 n. 3, 41, 51, 96, 107, 118
1:17	23, 119 n. 17
1:19	121, 122, 123
1:19–21	52
1:20	27
1:20–21	122
1:21	21, 22, 26, 27, 113
1:22	22, 25, 40
2:1	18, 23, 25, 26, 74
2:2	85
2:3	26, 42, 108, 121
2:4	18
2:5	108, 116 n/ 16
2:6	25
2:7	40, 42, 85
2:8	121
2:8–9	18, 40, 42
2:9	116 n. 16, 121
2:10	18, 40, 110
2:11	23, 75
2:11–12	27, 40, 75
2:12	18, 23, 28, 28 n. 50, 31 n. 20
2:13	40, 110
2:14	18
2:14–16	40, 42
2:15–16	18
2:16–17	74
2:17–18	85
2:18	18
2:20	27, 65, 108
2:21	25
2:22	123
2:23	121
3	86

3:1–4	123	1 Kings	
3:1–5	42	1:11–31	22
3:5	110	5:15	26 n. 40
3:7	19	17:1	21
3:9	24, 28, 42, 75, 76, 110	18:1–2	21
3:10	27, 40, 54, 76	22:4	35, 36, 41
3:11	23, 73, 74, 76, 85, 87		
3:12–13	23	2 Kings	
3:13	19 n. 14, 76	3:4–27	21
4:1	63	3:7	36
4:1–2	63	3:27	51
4:1–6	63		
4:1–12	57–72	Ezra	
4:2	64	2:1	30 n. 57
4:3	68	2:36–58	32 n. 66
4:3–6	64–65, 113	3:7	32 n. 68
4:5	25	4:4	30
4:5–6	110	6	33
4:6	19	6:8	32 n. 66
4:7–8	22, 65–66	6:9	32 n. 68
4:7–12	63	6:19–21	31
4:9–10	66–67	7:15–17, 22	32 n. 68
4:10	23, 25	7:26	31
4:11	24, 26	9:1	21, 31 n. 62
4:11–12	25, 27, 114, 121	9–10	31, 31 n. 62
4:12	24, 114		
4:13	19 n. 15, 23, 25, 26, 35	Nehemiah	
4:14–15	27	1	33
4:14–16	53	2:8	32 n. 68
4:14–17	121	4:1	30 n. 57
4:15	25	5	31, 32 n. 63
4:16	42	6:19	30 n. 57
4:16–17	123	6:20	30 n. 57
4:17	42, 114	7:6	30 n. 57
4:17–22	24, 26, 69	8:35	30 n. 57
		9	33
1 Samuel		9:4	30 n. 57
2:21	26 n. 41	9:35	33
14:47	21	9:36–37	33
22:3	114	10:6, 7, 8, 16	30 n. 57
25	80	10:29	31
		12:24, 45–46	32 n. 66
2 Samuel		13	134
8:2	21	13:1	21, 31 n. 62
21:1–14	21	13:23	31 n. 62

Nehemiah (cont.)
13:23–31					31, 31 n. 62

Job
1:1					28 n. 48
2:9–10					22
12:4					77
24:4, 21				18

Psalms
94:6					19
137					117

Proverbs
1:28					84
1–9					84
8:35					84
31					79 n.17, 81 n. 28, 84
31:3					78
31:10					73, 77, 78, 84, 85, 87
31:10–12				78
31:10–31				9, 23, 73–87
31:11–12				78
31:13					86
31:13–19				78
31:13–27				78
31:15					86
31:17					78
31:20–27				78
31:25					78
31:27					86
31:28–29				78
31:28–31				78
31:29					78
31:30–31				78
31:31					85

Ecclesiastes
2:14					26

Song of Solomon
5:7					23

Isaiah
1:21–23					18
10:1–12					18
15–16					21

Jeremiah
31:6					64
48					21

Lamentations
4:21					28 n. 49

Ezekiel
16:8					28 n. 50
25:8–11					21

Daniel
1					16 n. 3

Hosea
9:1					23

Amos
2:1–3					21
4:6–9					21
4:6–11					22
5:11–15					18
8:4–6					18

Micah
3:1–3					18

Malachi
2:16					28 n. 50

NEW TESTAMENT

Matthew
1:5					42

John
1					10 n. 40, 127

Modern Author Index

Ahn, Yong–Sung   4 n. 12, 125
Alexander, Ralph H.   62 n. 19, 62 n. 21
Alexander, T. Desmond   27 n. 44, 128
Ashcroft, Bill,   25 n. 38, 125
Bailey, Randall C.   11 n. 45, 125
Barker, Paul A.   22 n. 25, 125
Beal, Timothy K.   74 nn. 3–4, 131
Bells, Alice Odgen   89 n.1, 125
Berlin, Adele   25, 25 n. 37, 125
Bernstein, Moshe J.   19 n. 16, 125
Berquist, Jon L.   32, 32 nn. 64–65, 33 n. 69, 125
Bhabha, Homi K.   33 n. 71, 37–39, 42, 125, 130
Black, James   17 n. 10, 125
Bledstein, Adrien J.   53 n. 15, 54, 54 n. 17, 125
Block, Daniel I.   21 n. 23, 29 n. 52
Boer, Roland   2 n. 4, 3 n. 7, 4 n. 9, 4 nn. 11–12, 125, 126, 132
Braulik, Georg   17 n. 10, 125
Brenner, Athalya   51 n. 10, 52, 52 nn. 13–14, 89 n. 1, 106 n. 20, 107, 107 n. 26, 107 n. 33, 109, 109 nn. 34–37, 125
Brett, Mark G.   15, n. *, 16 n. 3, 120 n. 20, 126
Bush, Frederic William   21 n. 22, 105, 105 n. 17, 126
Camp, Claudia V.   80, 80 n. 21, 81 nn. 27–28, 84 n. 34, 126
Campbell, Edward F.   19 n. 14, 25 n. 35, 26 n. 42, 35 n. 1, 65, 65 n. 32, 126
Carmichael, Calum M.   19 n. 13, 126
Carrapiett, W. J. S.   61 n. 17, 70 n. 37, 126
Carroll, Sef   120 n. 20, 126
Chan, Kenneth Ka–lok   43 n. 28, 126
Chan, Kin Man   44 n. 31, 126
Cheung, Tony   46 n. 38, 126
Chia, Philip   2 n. 4, 16 n. 3, 126
Childs, Peter   17 n. 9, 127
Chirichigno, Gregory C.   20 n. 21, 127
Chittister, Joan   89 n. 1, 127
Christensen, Duane L.   57 n. 1, 62 n. 18, 127
Chu, Julie L. C.   89 n. 1, 90 n. 2, 127
Clarke, Sarah   101 n. 5, 127
Clines, David J. A.   17 n. 10, 28 n. 49, 127
Collins, John J.   38, 38 n. 16, 127
Coorey, Phillip   102 n. 9, 127
Crowell, Bradley L.   15, 15 n. 1, 127
D'Sa, Francis X.   10 n. 40, 127
Daide   50 n. 8, 127
Davis, Ellen F.   82 n. 31, 127
DeSilva, David A.   16 n. 3, 127
Donaldson, Laura E.   90 n. 2, 127
Dozeman, Thomas B.   25 n. 39, 127
Dube, Musa W.   90 n. 2, 127
Dyk, Janet W.   19 n. 17, 127
Eskenazi, Tamara C.   30 n. 54, 32 n. 67, 112 n. 5, 127–28
Farmer, Kathleen A.   81 n. 25, 84 n. 41, 128
Fewell, Danna N.   18 n. 12, 112 n. 4, 114 n. 8, 114 n. 10, 115 n. 11, 128
Fischer, Imtraud   108 n. 30, 128
Fishbane, Michael   31 n. 62, 128
Foskett, Mary F.   5 nn. 13–14, 5 n. 16, 9 n. 33, 128

Freire, Paulo 124 n. 27, 128
Frymer–Kensky, Tikva Simone
    30 n. 54, 128
Gafney, Wil 121, 121 n. 4, 128
Gilhodes 59 n. 9, 60 n. 13, 60 n. 15,
    128
Gillard, Julia 102
Gitay, Zefira 52, 52 n. 14, 128
Glover, Neil 25 n. 34, 128
Goh, Elaine W. F. 9, 14, 24 n. 28,
    73–87, 128
Goswell, Greg 33 n. 70, 33 n. 72,
    128
Goulder, Michael D. 17 n. 10, 128
Gow, Murray D. 23 n. 26, 27,
    27 n. 44, 128
Griffiths, Emma 104 n. 14, 128
Griffiths, Gareth 25 n. 38, 128
Gun, Maru Tang 60, 60 n. 14
Gun, N–Gan Tang 60 n. 11
Gunn, David M. 18 n. 12, 112 n. 4,
    114 n. 8, 114 n. 10, 115 n. 11, 128
Gutstein, Naphtali 84 n. 35, 129
Halton, Charles 20 n. 19, 23 n. 27,
    129
Hanson, Ola 58 n. 5, 129
Harm, Harry J. 19 n. 17, 129
Havea, Jione 1, 3, 5 n. 15, 10 n. 39,
    14, 111–24, 120 n. 20, 129
Hawkins, Tom R. 78 n. 14, 84 n. 35,
    129
Hoglund, Kenneth G. 30 n. 58,
    79 n. 20, 129
Holladay, William L. 63 n. 23,
    64 n. 28
Holmstedt, Robert D. 105,
    105 n. 18, 106, 106 n. 24, 129
Huang, Wei 7 n. 26, 130
Hubbard Jr., Robert L. 24 n. 31,
    29 n. 52, 65 n. 31, 66 n. 33, 74 n. 2,
    75 n. 5, 77 n. 10, 130
Huddart, David 38, 39 n. 18,
    39 n. 21, 130
Huwiler, Elizabeth 78 n. 11, 133
Ja, Kumje Roi 70, 70 n. 38, 130

Japhet, Sara 30 n. 55, 130
Kalmin, Richard 62 n. 20, 130
Keita, Schadrac 19 n. 17, 130
Kim, Yong–Bock 11 n. 42, 130
Kinukawa, Hisako 13, 13 n. 53, 130
Koosed, Jennifer L. 111 n. 3,
    112 n. 4, 118, 130
Kstes, Judith A. 89 n. 1, 91 n 3, 130
Kuan, Jeffrey Kah–Jin 130
Kutsch, E. 62 n. 18, 63 n. 24, 130
Kwok, Pui–lan 3 n. 8, 7 n. 25,
    12 n. 49, 13, 13 n. 51, 89 n. 1,
    90 n. 2, 122 n. 25, 130–31
Kwon, Oh–Young 11 n. 41, 131
LaCocque, André 6, 17 n. 10,
    24 nn. 29, 24 n. 32, 30 n. 54,
    89 n. 1, 94 n. 6, 131
Lau, Peter H. W. 1, 12, 14, 15–34,
    19 n. 18, 25 n. 36, 30 n. 59,
    31 n. 61, 131
Leach, Edmund R. 57 n. 3, 68,
    68 n. 35, 131
Lee, Archie C. C. 7, 8 nn. 27, 8 n. 32,
    44, 131
Lee, Eunny 8 nn. 15–16, 105 n. 15,
    131
Lee, Kyung Sook 8 n. 31, 122 n. 26,
    131
Lee, Yeong Mee 7 n. 23, 131
Levine, Amy–Jill 49 n. 7, 54,
    54 n. 16, 89 n. 1, 131
Li, Chichang 44 n. 32, 131
Li, Pungga Ja 59 n. 10
Liew, Tat–siong Benny 5 n. 13,
    11 n. 46, 125, 132
Linafelt, Tod 74 nn. 3–4,
    107 n. 27, 131
Lyn, Tan Ee 45 n. 36, 132
Lyons, Ellen Louise 79 n. 20,
    80 n. 22, 85 n. 44, 132
Masenya, Madipoane 82 n. 29,
    89 n. 1, 90 n. 2, 132
Matthews, Victor H. 30 n. 54, 132
McCreesh, Thomas P. 84 nn. 35–36,
    84 nn. 39, 84 n. 42, 132

McKane, William   81 n. 27, 132
Melanchthon, Monica Jyotsna
    4 n. 9, 11 n. 43, 132
Mettinger, Tryggve N. D.   27 n. 46,
    132
Meyers, Carol L.   79 18–19,
    89 n. 1, 132
Miles, Johnny   4 n. 11, 132
Milgrom, Jacob   20 n. 21, 132
Miller, Patrick D.   27 n. 45, 133
Murphy, Roland E.   78 n. 11,
    83 n. 32, 84 n. 37, 84 n. 43, 132–33
Nadar, Sarojini   90 n.2, 133
Nelavala, Surekha   6, 14, 89–97, 133
Nicholson, Ernest W.   30 n. 55, 133
Nielsen, Kirsten   17 n. 10, 21 n. 23,
    24 n. 30, 26 n. 44, 133
Niles, Damayanthi M. A.   11 n. 44,
    11 n. 46, 133
Nu, Roi   12, 14, 57–72, 133
O'Connor, Kathleen M.   133
Pa, Anna May Say   9 n. 36, 90 n. 2,
    133
Pardes, Ilana   89 n. 1, 95 n. 7,
    97 n. 9, 133
Pattel–Gray, Anne   6, 6 n. 21, 133
Perdue, Leo G.   77 n. 9, 79 n. 20,
    80 nn. 22–23, 133
Phillips, Anthony   19 n. 13, 133
Phillips, Janet 100 n. 3, 102 n. 6, 133
Pieris, Aloysius   8 n. 30, 133
Pomfret, James   45 n. 36, 133
Raja, Maria Arul   9 n. 37, 133
Rao, Naveen   11, 11 n. 47, 12, 134
Rashkow, Ilona   51 n. 10, 106 n. 20,
    106 n. 23, 107 n. 25, 108 n. 32, 134
Rees, Anthony   3, 14, 99–110,
    116 n. 14, 134
Reimer, Gail Twersky   89 n. 1, 134
Rogerson, John W.   32 n. 63, 134
Rongpei, Wang   48 nn. 5–6,
    51 n. 11, 134
Rudd, Kevin   101–103
Said, Edward W.   99, 99 n. 1, 134

Sakenfeld, Katharine Doob   37 n. 7,
    40, 40 nn. 23–24, 42 n. 26, 75, 75 n.
    6, 79 n. 17, 83, 83 n. 33, 85,
    85 nn. 45–46, 87, 90 n. 2, 105 n. 15,
    134
Sals, Ulrike   38, 38 nn. 12–15, 134
Sassoon, Jack M.   74 n. 4, 134
Saysell, Csilla   31 n. 64, 134
Scott, James George   58, 58 n. 7, 134
Se, Lahtaw Gum   60 n. 12
Segovia, Fernando F.   16, 16 n. 5,
    38 n. 8, 134
Shanahan, Dennis   103 n. 13, 134
Smith, Mark S.   36–37, 36 n. 3, 41,
    41 n. 25, 134
Smith–Christopher, Daniel L.
    31 n. 62, 33 n. 72, 134
Spivak, Gayatri Chakravorty   1 n. 2,
    2, 3 n. 6, 134
Stanton, Elizabeth C.   107, 107 n. 26,
    107. n. 28, 134
Sugirtharajah, R. S.   1 n. 1, 2 n. 3,
    2 n. 5, 4, 4 n. 10, 6 n. 18, 12 n. 50,
    13, 16, 16 n. 4, 135
Suqing, Lin   54 n. 18, 135
Swarup, Paul   10 n. 40, 135
Tate, W. Randolph   15 n. 2, 16,
    16 n. 7, 135
Taylor, F. J.   64 n. 29, 135
Tegenfeldt   57 n. 3, 59 n. 8, 135
Tesoo, Yim   7 n. 26, 11 n. 42, 135
Thiselton, Anthony C.   16, 16 n. 6,
    135
Tiffin, Helen   25 n. 38, 125
Timmer, Daniel C.   16 n. 3, 28 n. 51,
    135
Tolbert, Mary Ann   16 n. 5, 134
Tong, Sin–lung   12, 14, 35–46
Torn, Susan Reimer   89 n. 1, 135
Tran, Mai–Anh Le   9, 9 n. 33, 135
Trible, Phyllis   89 n. 1, 94 n. 5, 106,
    106 n. 21, 136
Trieu, Rosa   43 n. 29, 136
van Wolde, Ellen   17 n. 10, 19 n. 15,
    136

von Rad, Gerhard   57 n. 2, 136
Walker, Ting   102 n. 11, 136
Waltke, Bruce K.   77 n. 10,
    78 n. 13, 136
Wang, Tai Il   10 n. 41, 136
Wawm, Labang La   59 n. 10
Weber, Jean Jacques   17 n. 9
Weems, Renita J.   89 n. 1, 136
Weinfeld, Moshe   29 n. 52, 136
Wickeri, Philip L.   7 n. 22, 136
Williams, Patrick   17 n. 9, 127
Williamson, H. G. M.   32 n. 66, 136
Wolters, Albert M.   78 n. 16,
    84 n. 42, 136
Wong, Wai Ching   6, 6 nn. 19–20,
    136
Yamaguchi, Satoko   8 n. 29, 136
Yan, Lin   9–10, 47–55
Yee, Gale A.   5 n. 14, 136
Yoder, Christine Roy   78 n. 12,
    81 n. 26, 137
Yoo, Yoon Jong   7 n. 23, 131
Zakovitch, Yair   17 n. 10, 19 n. 14,
    21 n. 24, 24 nn. 30, 24 n. 33,
    26 n. 40, 95 n. 8, 137
Zevit, Ziony   30 n. 54, 137
Ziegler, Yael   37, 37 n. 5, 137

www.ingramcontent.com/pod-product-compliance
Lightning Source LLC
Chambersburg PA
CBHW031315150426
43191CB00005B/242